My
Number
Book

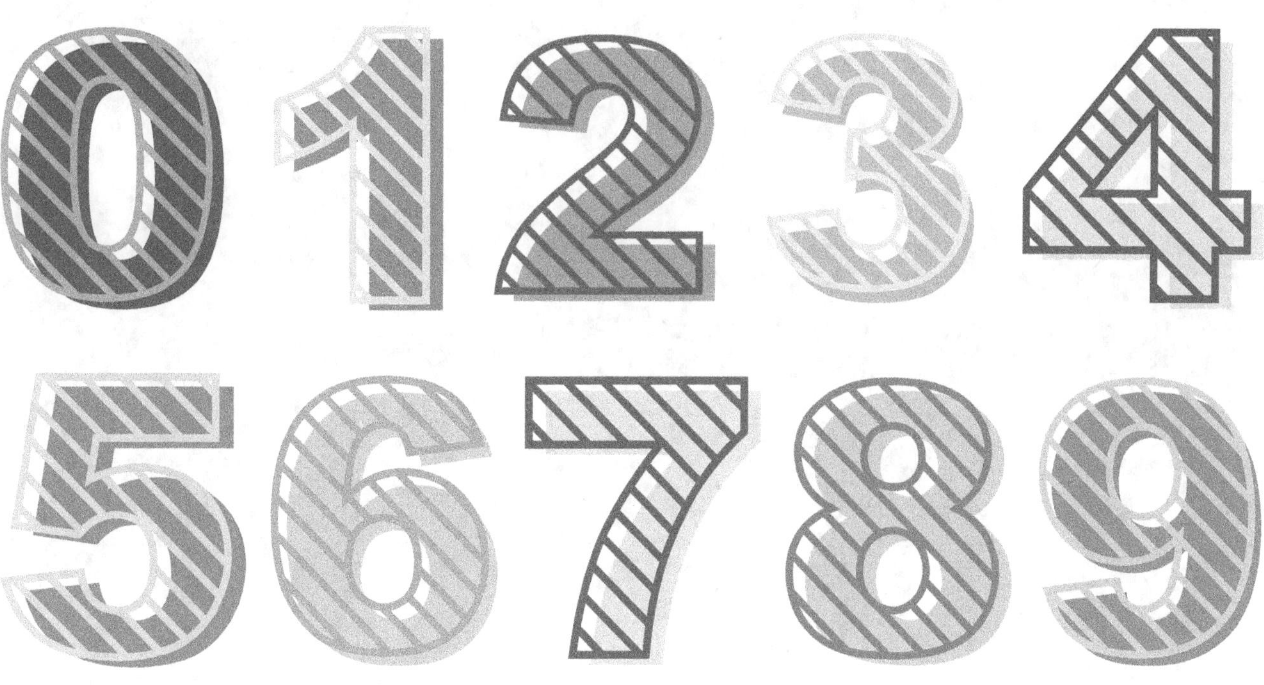

Name

zero

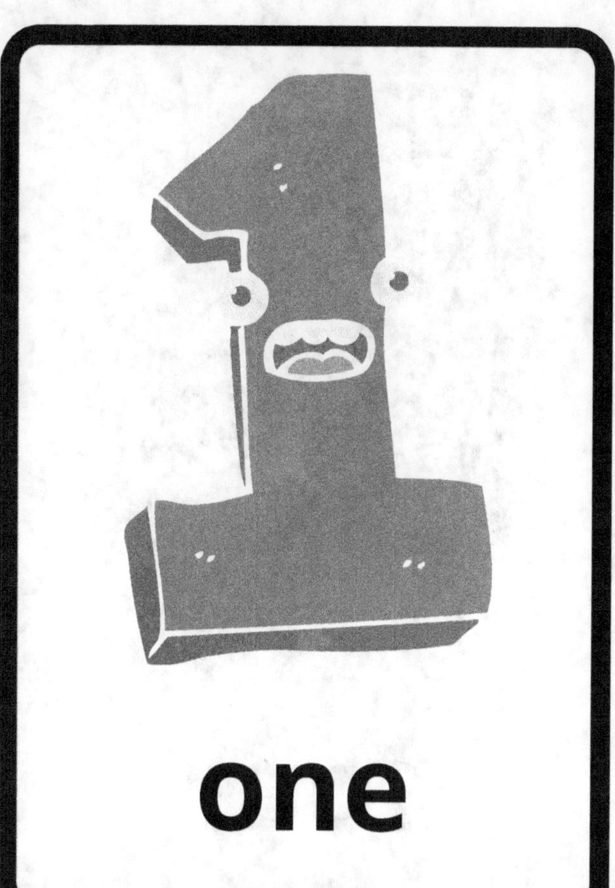

one

two

three

four

five

six

seven

eight

nine

Name: _________

Number Tracing

Print, Laminate & Trace

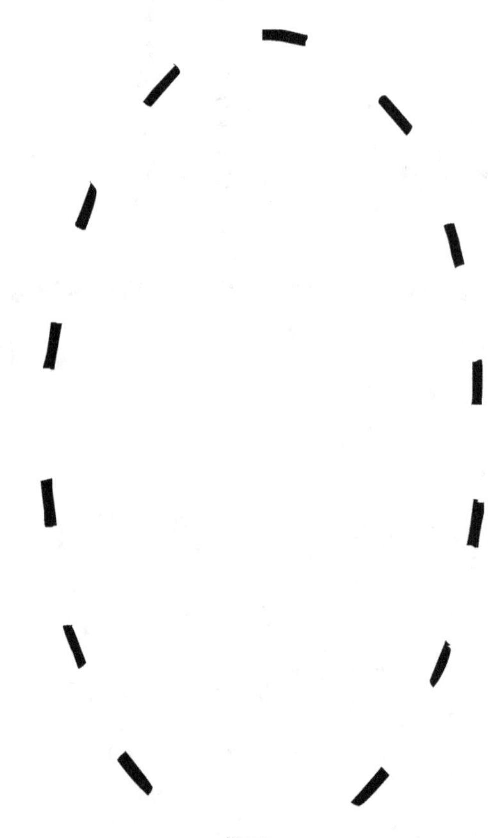

Number Tracing

Print, Laminate & Trace

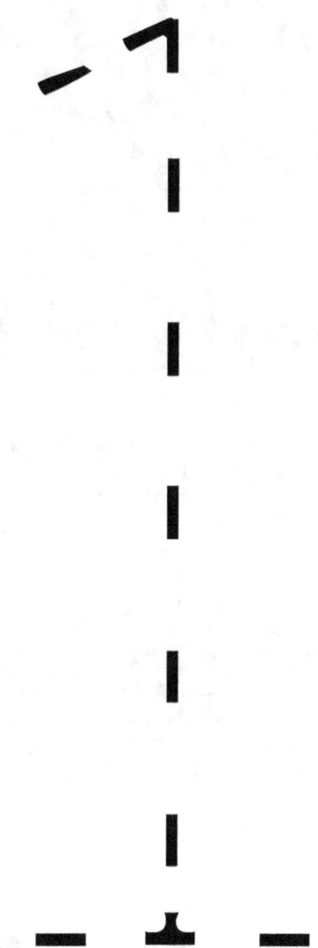

Number Tracing

Print, Laminate & Trace

Number Tracing

Print, Laminate & Trace

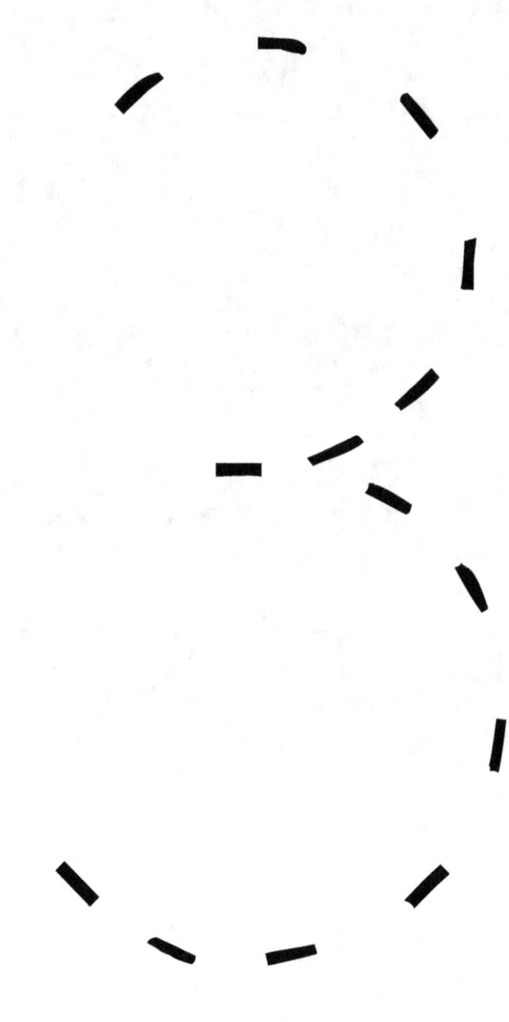

Number Tracing

Print, Laminate & Trace

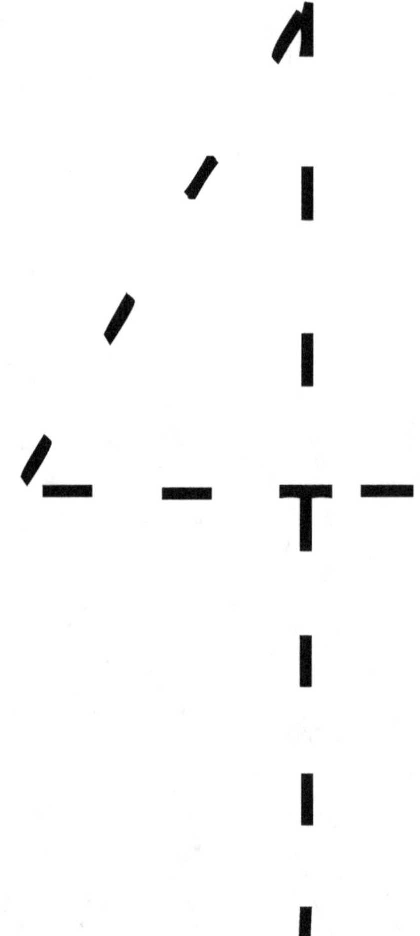

Number Tracing

Print, Laminate & Trace

Name: ________________

Number Tracing

Print, Laminate & Trace

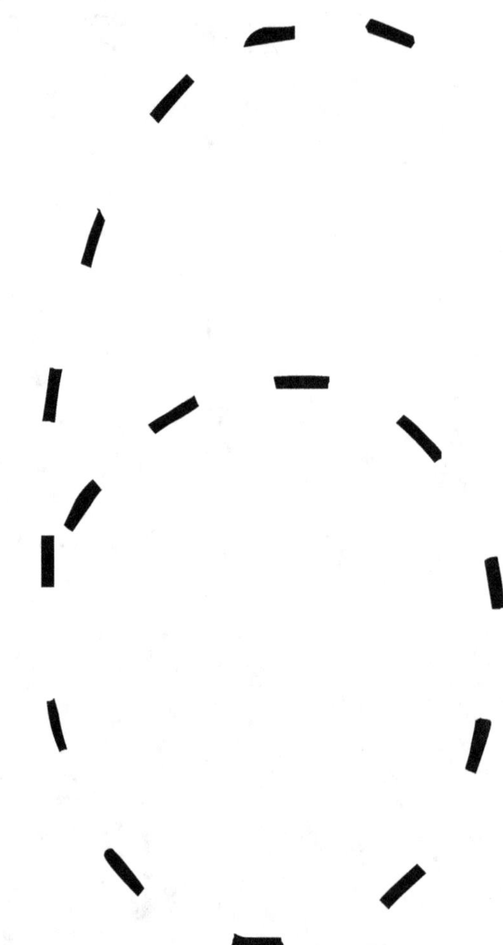

Number Tracing

Print, Laminate & Trace

Number Tracing

Print, Laminate & Trace

Number Tracing

Print, Laminate & Trace

Tracing
Numbers

Trace N° 0 & count...

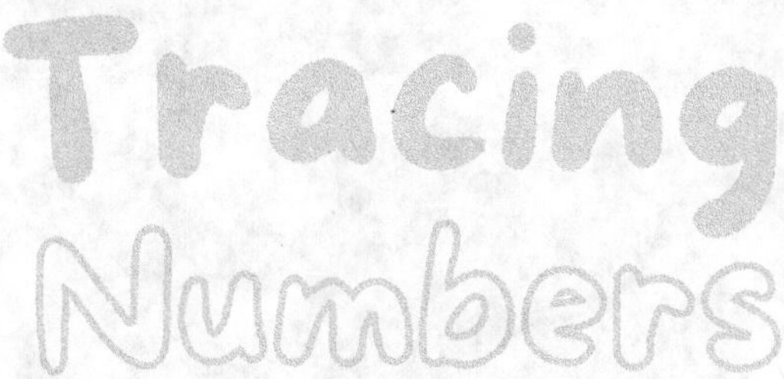

Tracing
Numbers

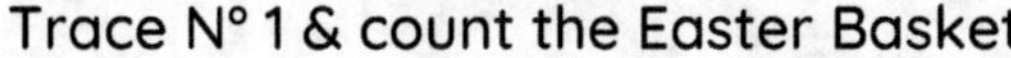

Trace N° 1 & count the Easter Basket

Tracing
Numbers

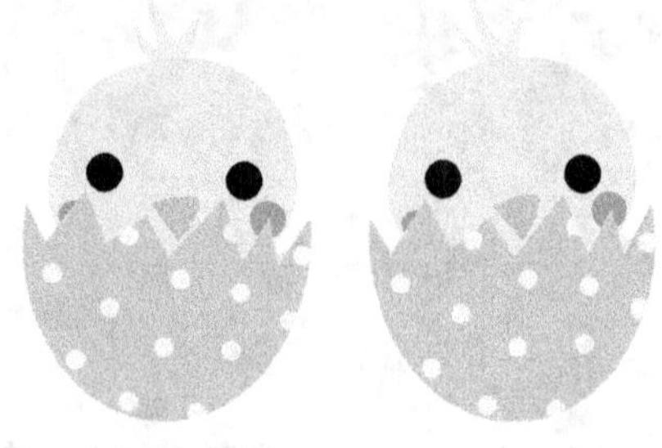

Trace Nº 2 & count the Easter Chicks

Tracing
Numbers

Trace N° 3 & count the Easter Eggs

Tracing
Numbers

Trace N° 4 & count the Butterflies

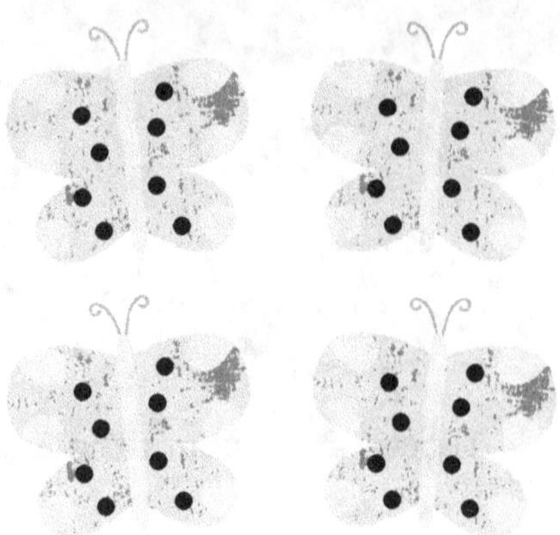

Tracing Numbers

Trace Nº 5 & count the Easter Chicks

Tracing
Numbers

Trace N° 5 & count the Easter Chicks

Tracing

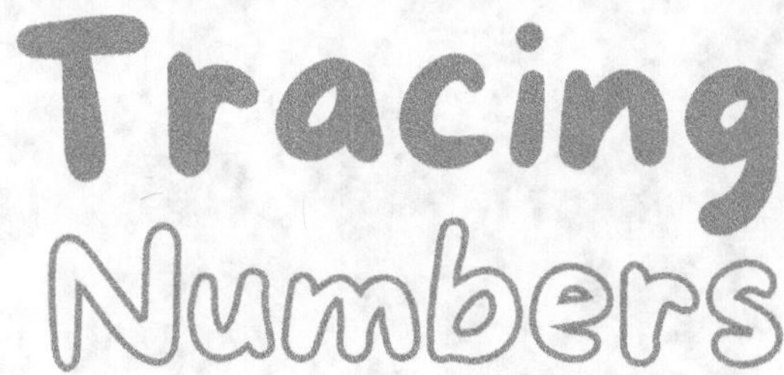

Numbers

Trace N° 7 & count the Tulips

Tracing
Numbers

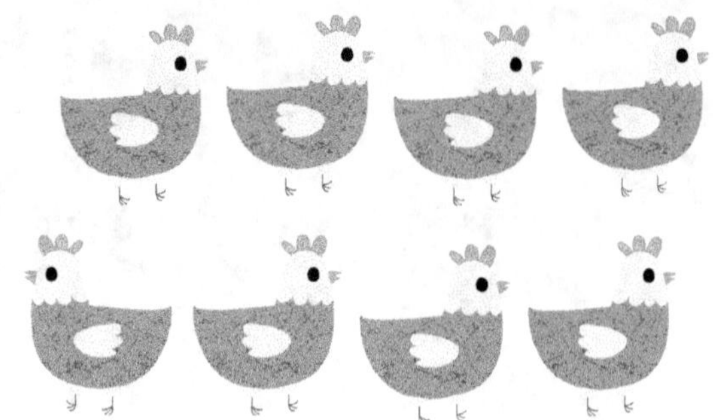

Trace Nº 8 & count the Easter Hens

Tracing
Numbers

Trace N° 9 & count the Easter Bunnies

DIRECTIONS: TRACE THE WORDS AND NUMBERS BELOW.

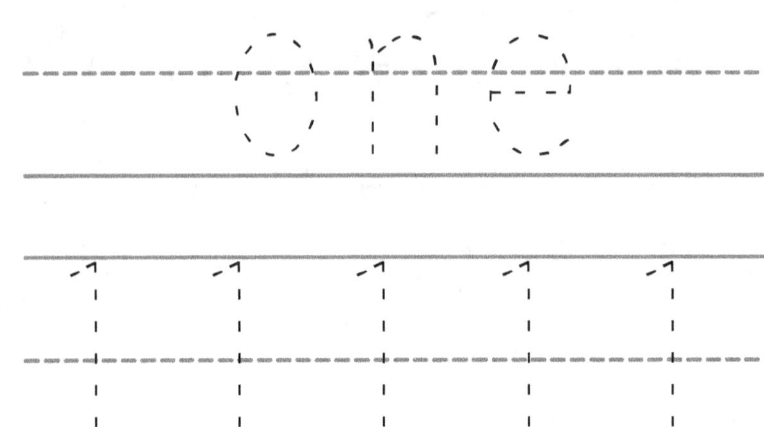

COLOR ONE STAR:

CIRCLE THE ONES:

1	3	5
4	2	1
6	1	8
1	7	1
2	1	4

DIRECTIONS: TRACE THE WORDS AND NUMBERS BELOW.

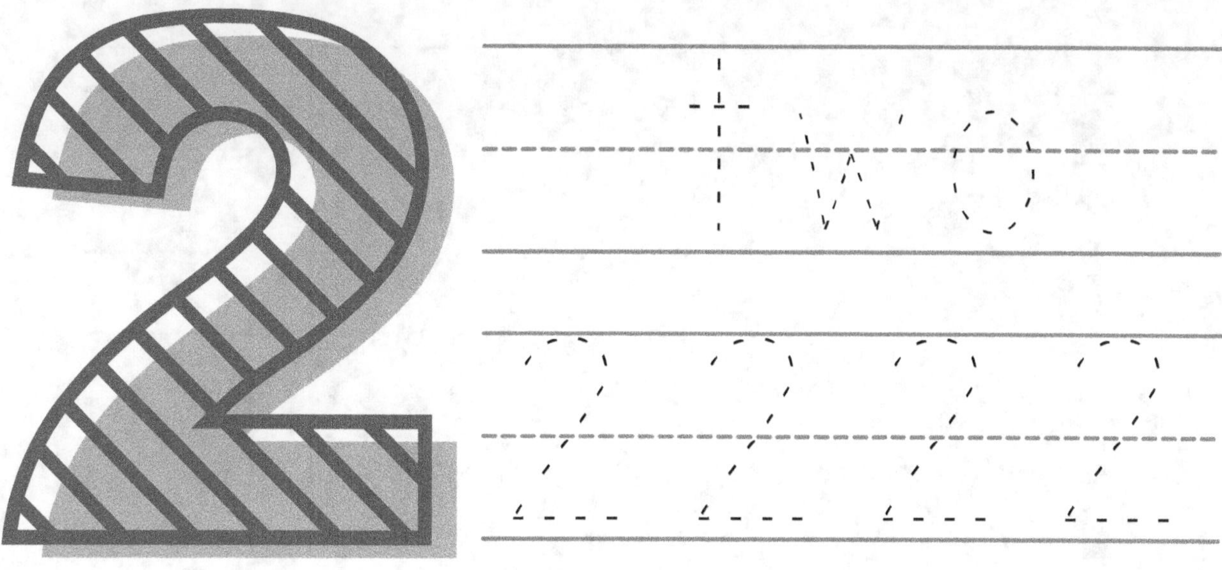

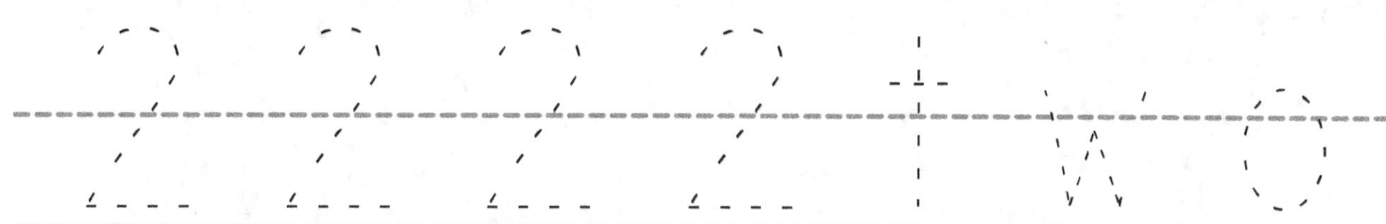

<table>
<tr>
<td>

COLOR TWO TRIANGLES:

</td>
<td>

CIRCLE THE TWOS:

2	3	5
4	2	1
6	1	2
1	2	1
2	1	4

</td>
</tr>
</table>

DIRECTIONS: TRACE THE WORDS AND NUMBERS BELOW.

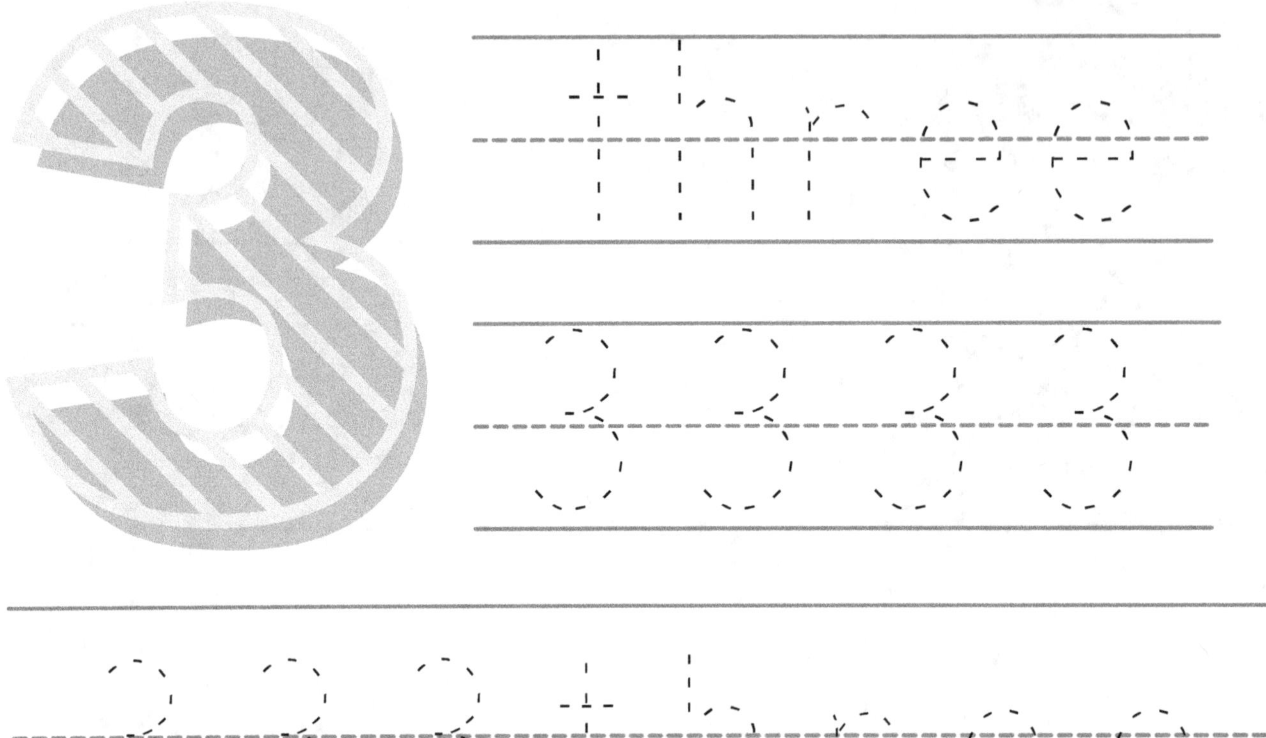

CIRCLE THE THREES:

2	3	5
4	2	3
3	1	2
3	5	1
6	3	4

Name: _______________________

DIRECTIONS: TRACE THE WORDS AND NUMBERS BELOW.

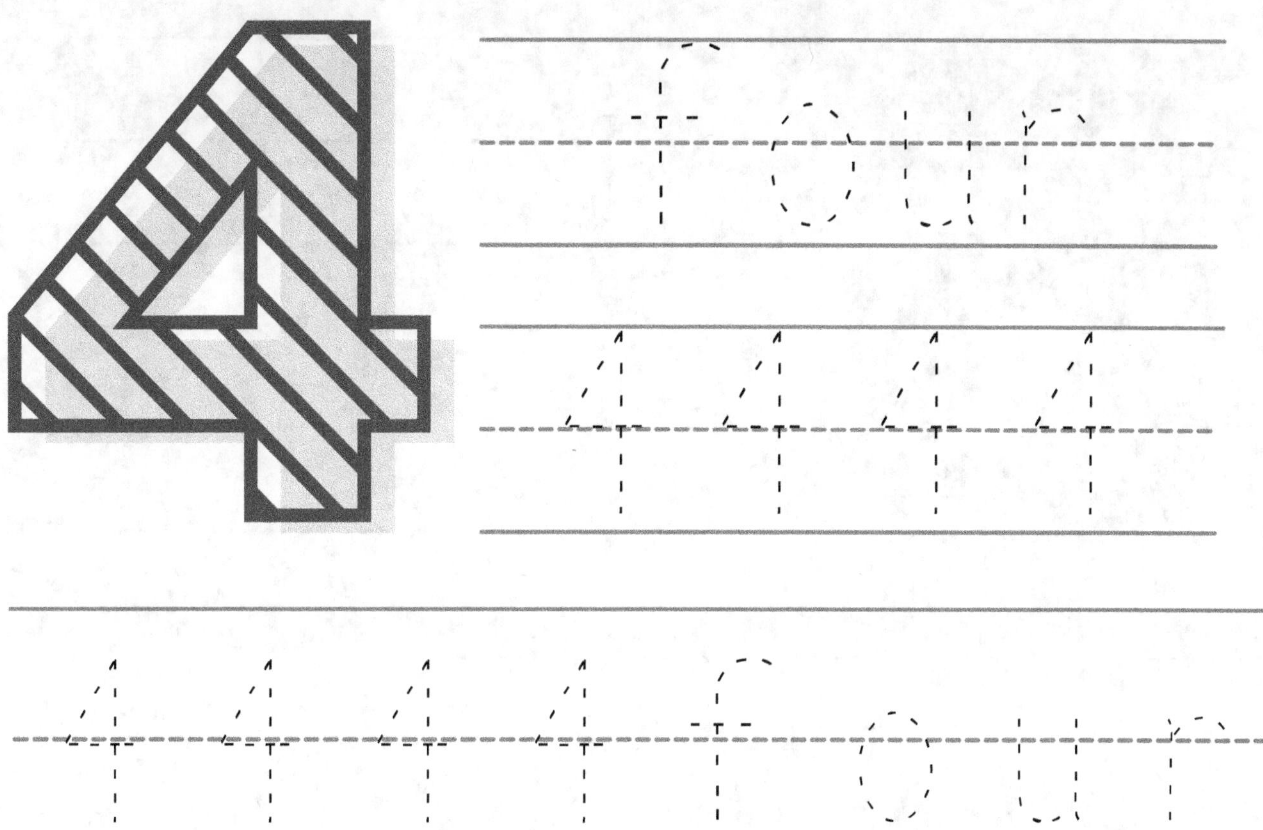

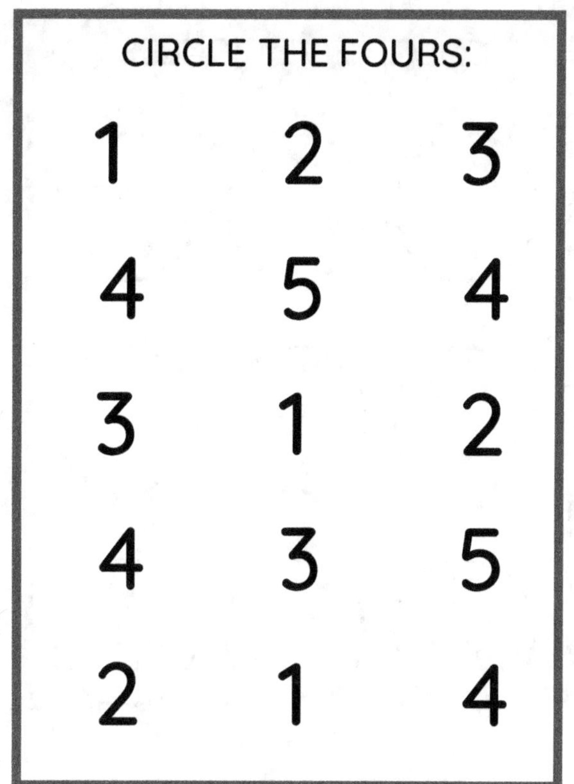

DIRECTIONS: TRACE THE WORDS AND NUMBERS BELOW.

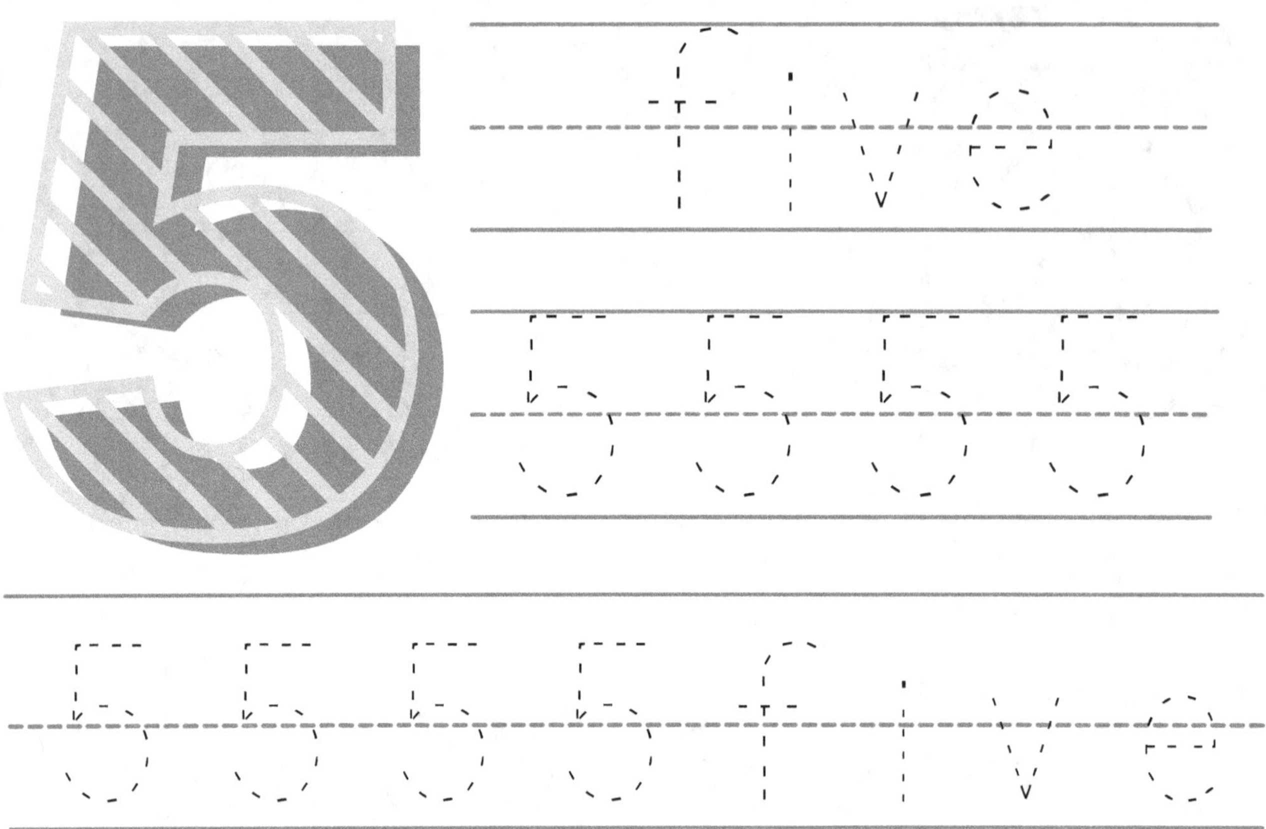

DIRECTIONS: TRACE THE WORDS AND NUMBERS BELOW.

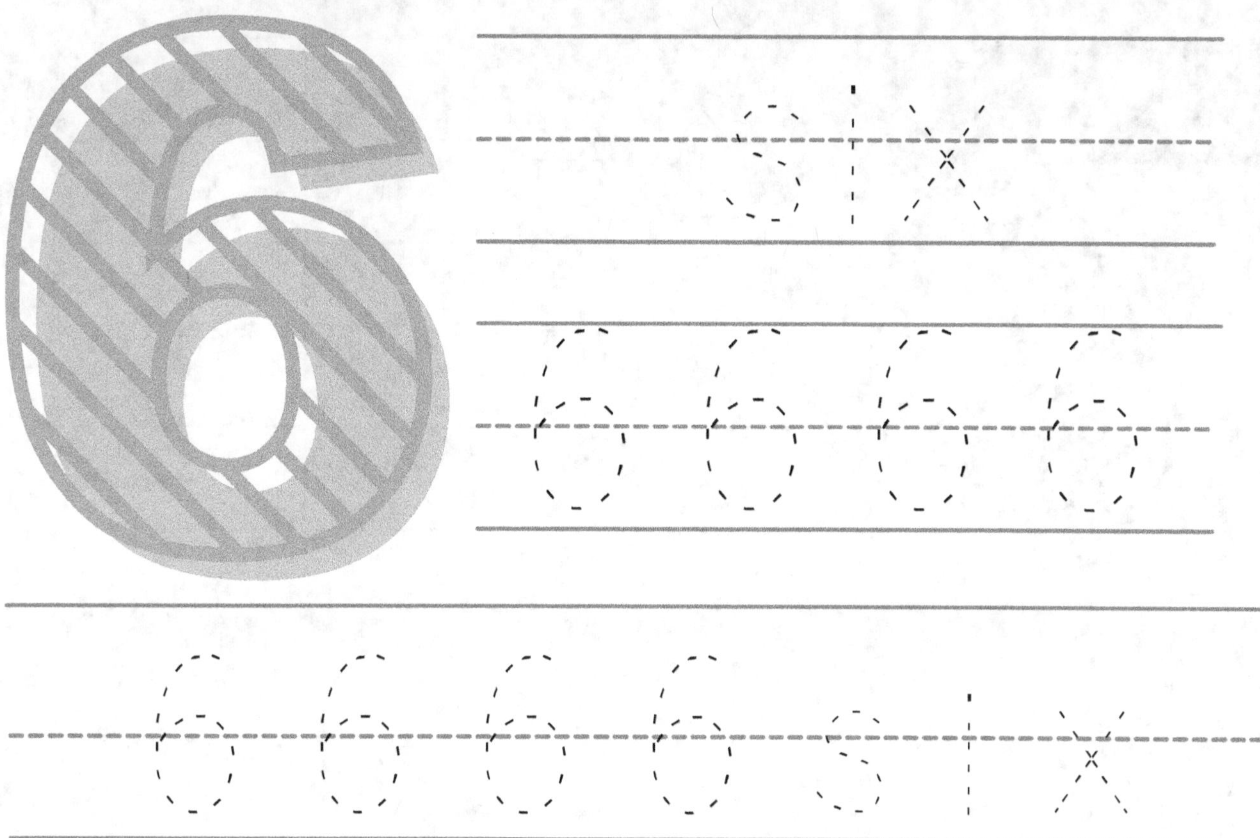

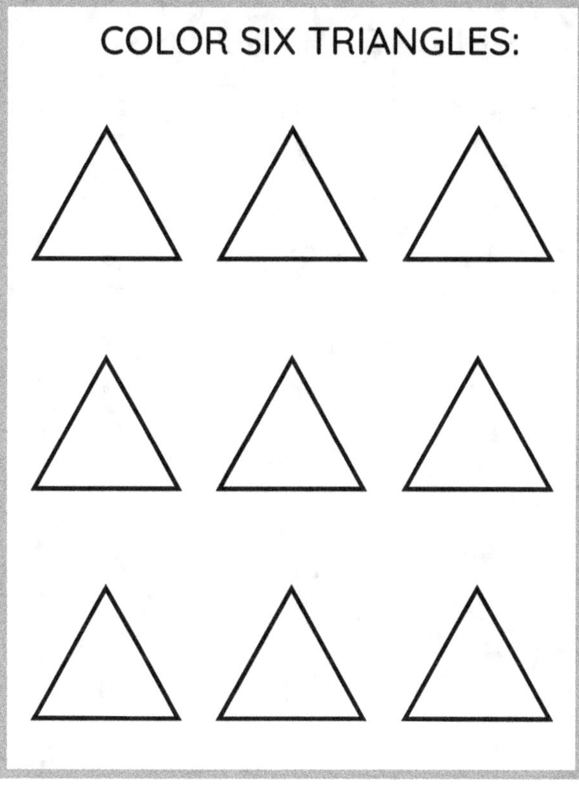

COLOR SIX TRIANGLES:

CIRCLE THE SIXES

5	6	3
1	2	6
6	5	4
4	3	6
2	6	1

DIRECTIONS: TRACE THE WORDS AND NUMBERS BELOW.

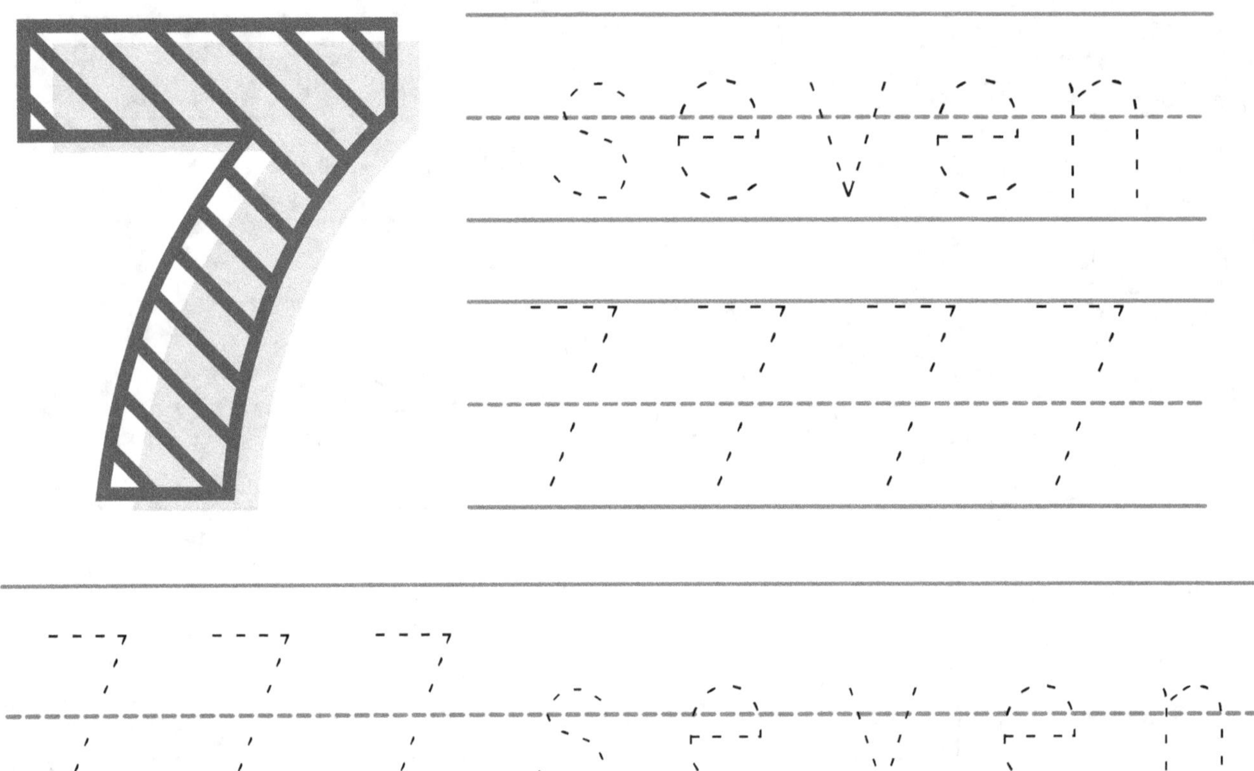

DIRECTIONS: TRACE THE WORDS AND NUMBERS BELOW.

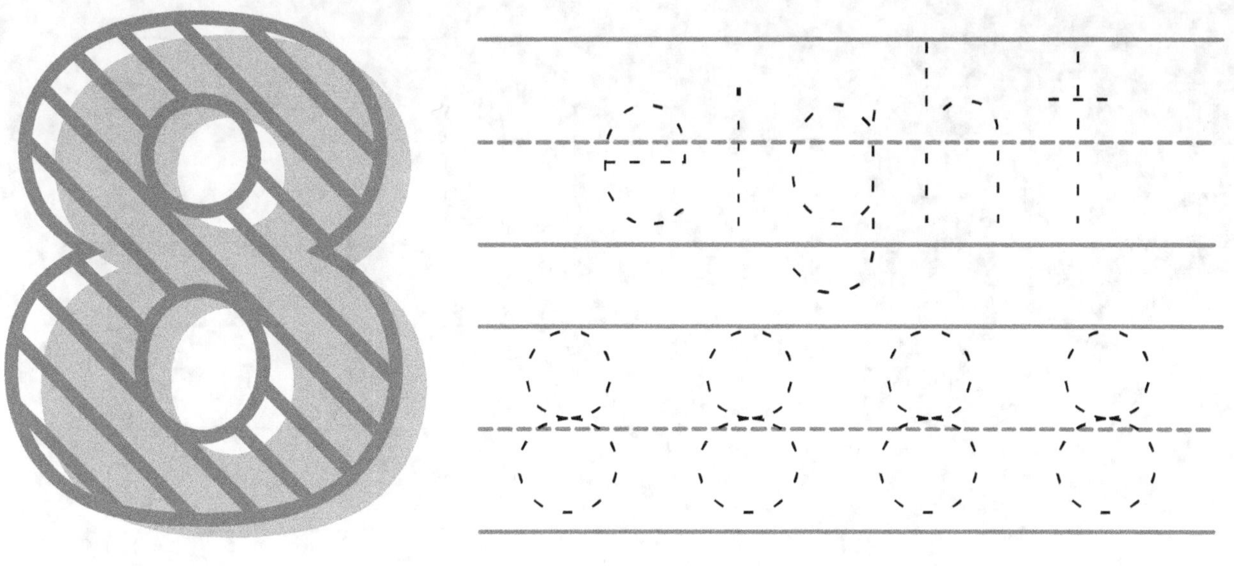

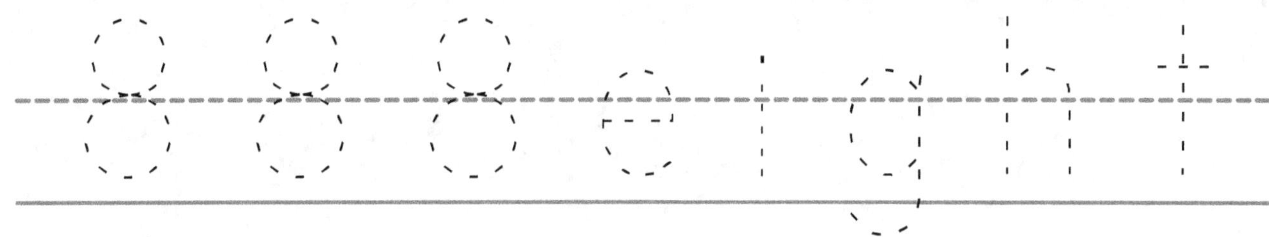

CIRCLE THE EIGHTS:

1	8	3
4	5	8
8	6	2
4	3	8
2	5	1

DIRECTIONS: TRACE THE WORDS AND NUMBERS BELOW.

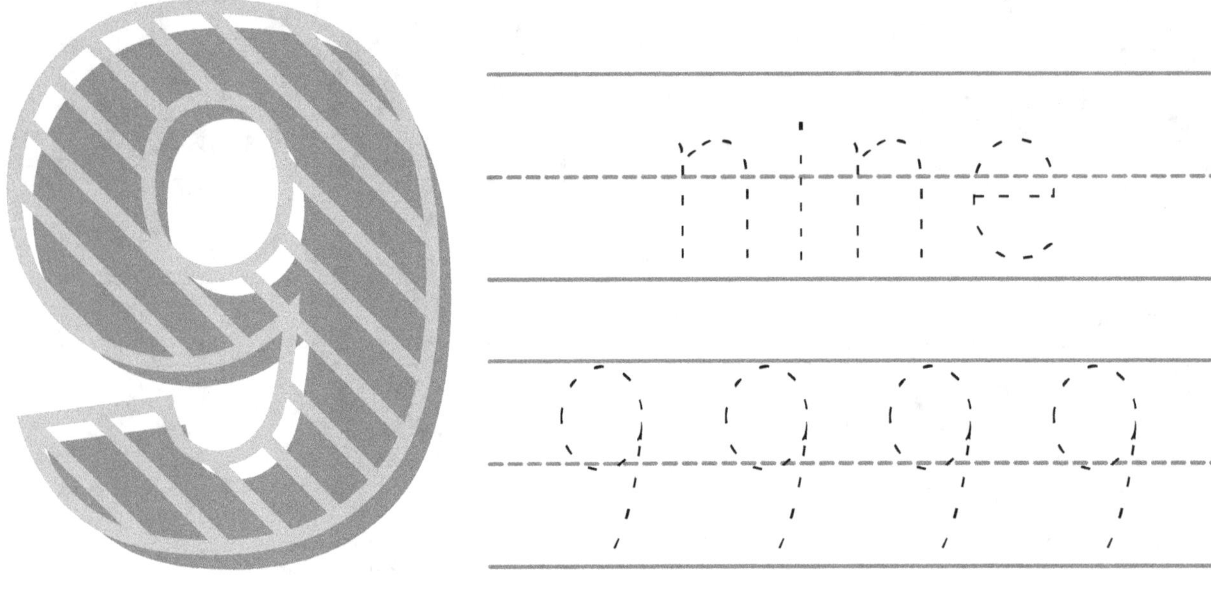

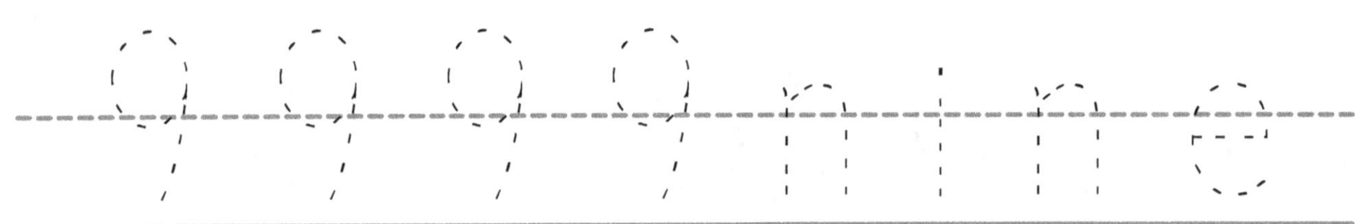

COLOR NINE HATS:

CIRCLE THE NINES:

9	8	6
4	7	9
8	6	9
4	9	8
9	5	1

Name: ______________________   Section: ______________________

Teacher: ______________________   Date: ______________________

TRACING NUMBERS

Trace the numbers in the boxes.

1			1	1
2	2	2	2	2
3			3	3
4			4	4
5			5	5

Name:

Section:

Teacher:

Date:

Tracing Numbers

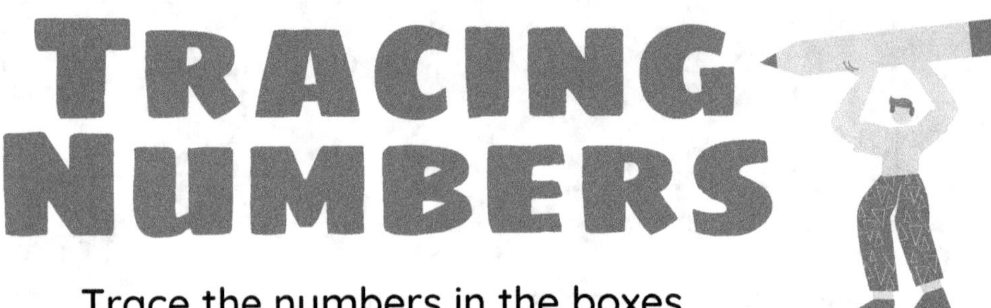

Trace the numbers in the boxes.

6	6	6	6	6
7	7	7	7	7
8	8	8	8	8
9	9	9	9	9
0	0	0	0	0

I CAN WRITE NUMBERS

Practice writing your numbers. Trace the first three then
complete the row on your own.

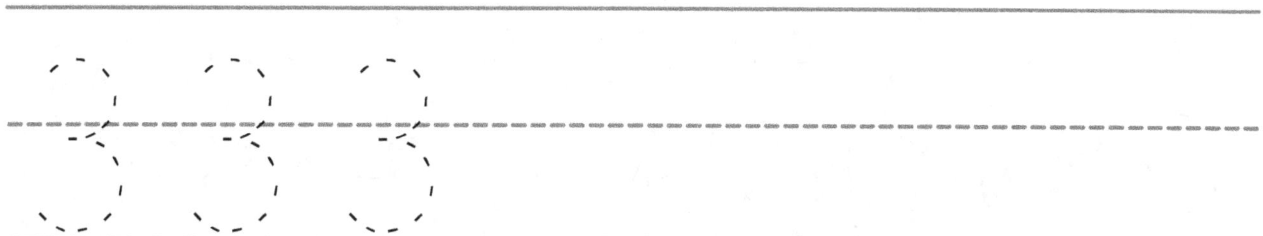

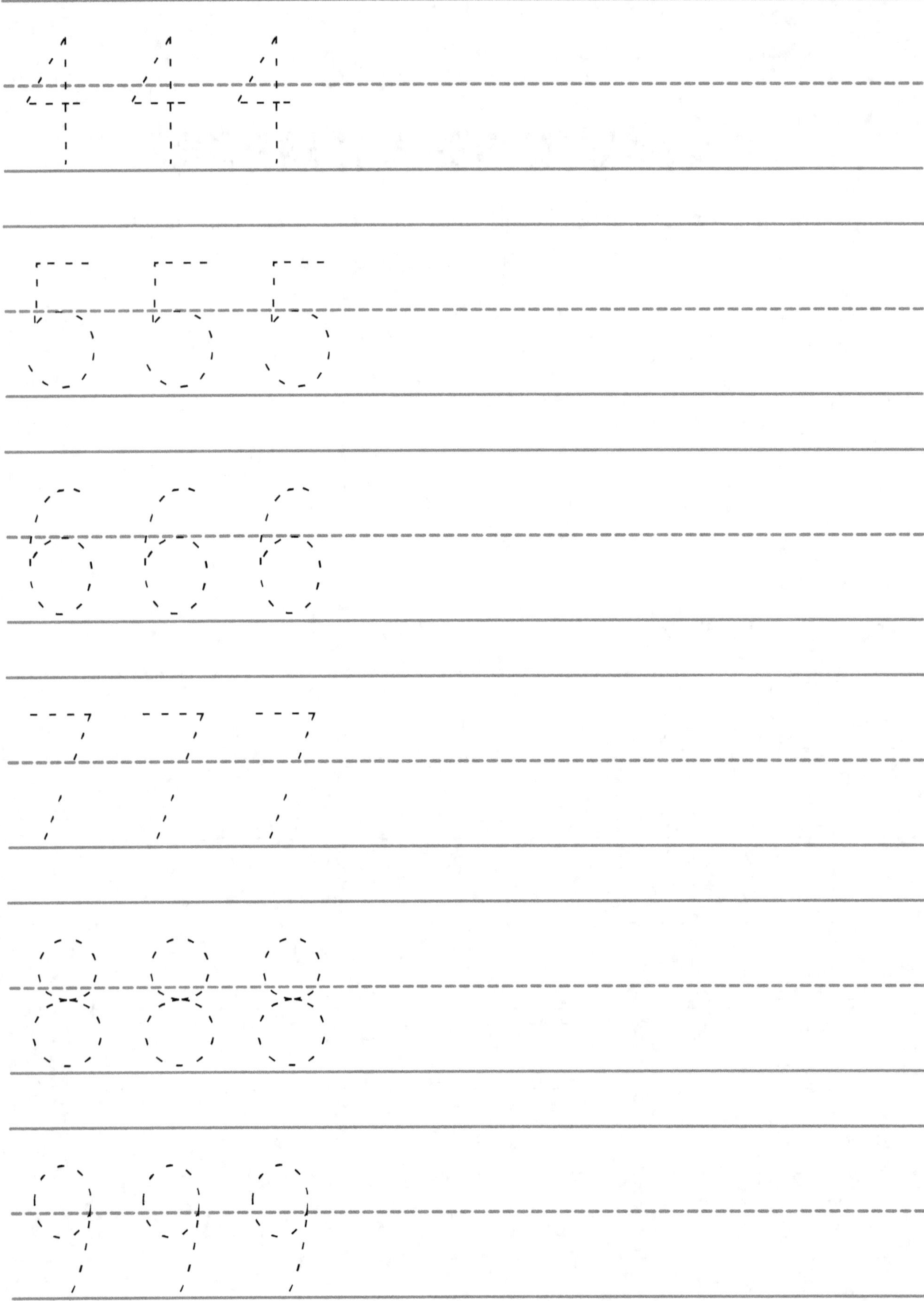

Name:

Section:

Date:

Teacher:

Number Values

Color the number that has the bigger value

5	8	4	5
6	0	3	2
9	5	4	7
8	2	6	1

GREATER OR LESS THAN

Compare the numbers and write <, >, or =

10 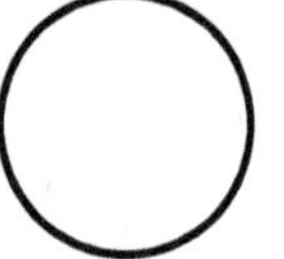 8	1  10
6 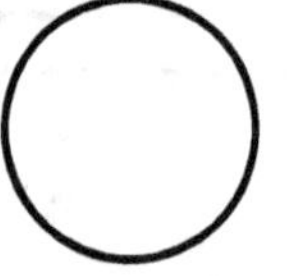 7	3  3
5 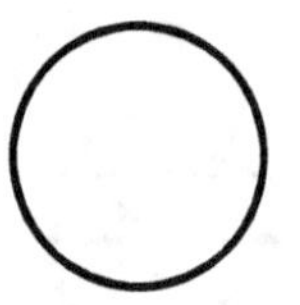 5	0  8
3 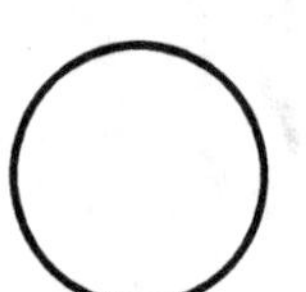 9	7 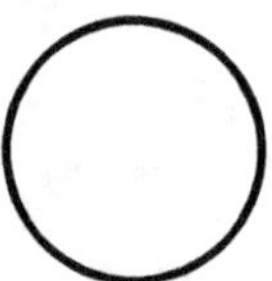 9
4 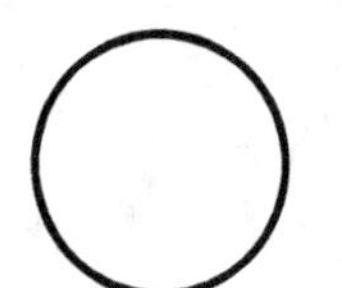 2	6 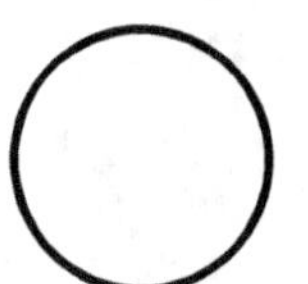 4

Before and After

Write the numbers that come before
and after the number in the middle.

8	**9**	10			**7**	
6					**1**	
	3				**3**	
	5				**5**	
	2				**4**	
	8				**2**	

The Number Zero

DIRECTIONS: TRACE THE WORDS AND NUMBERS BELOW TO PRACTICE THE NUMBER ZERO! WHEN YOU'RE FINISHED COLOR THE NUMBER.

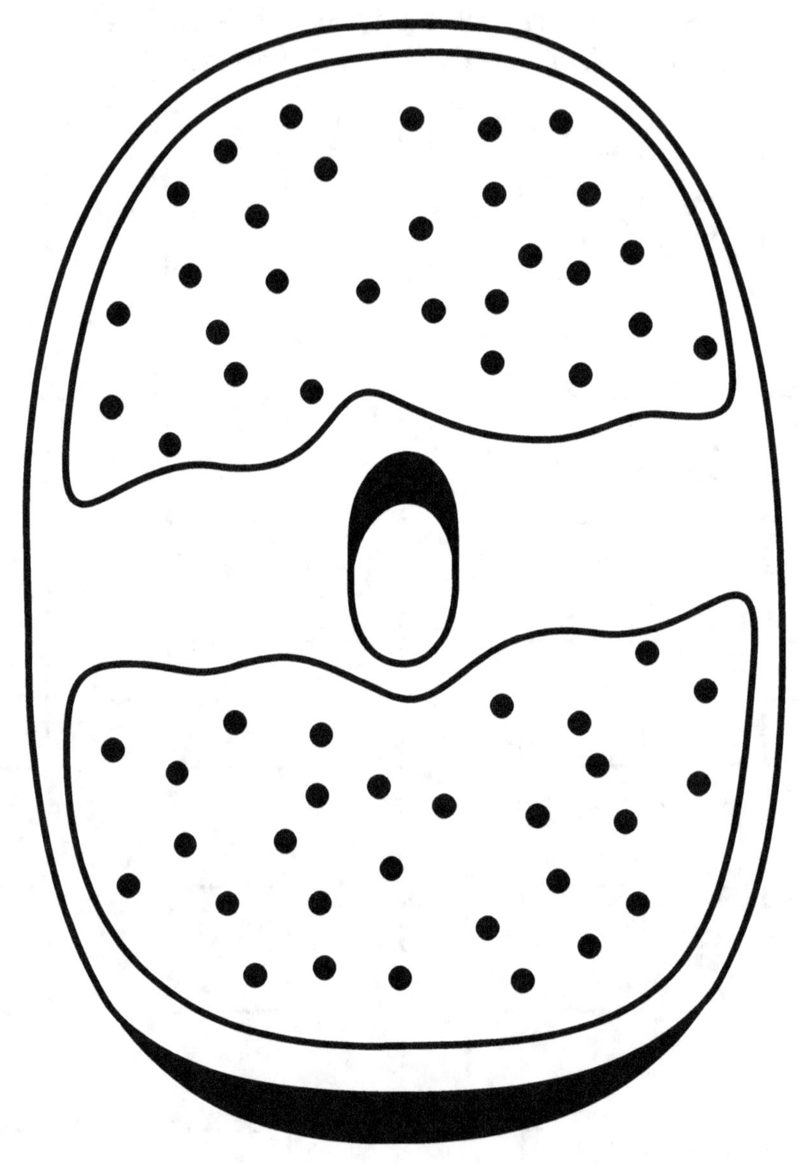

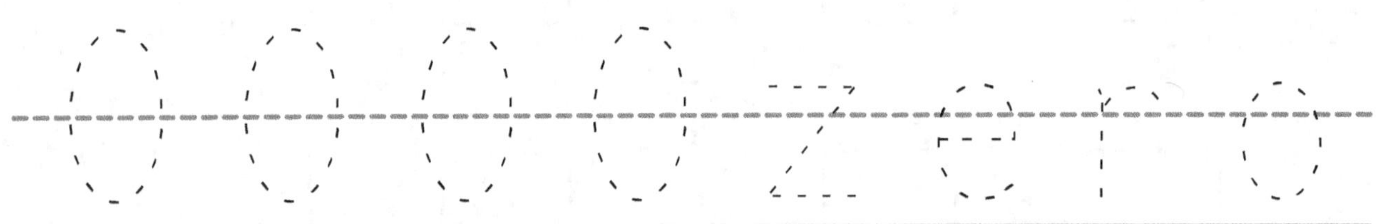

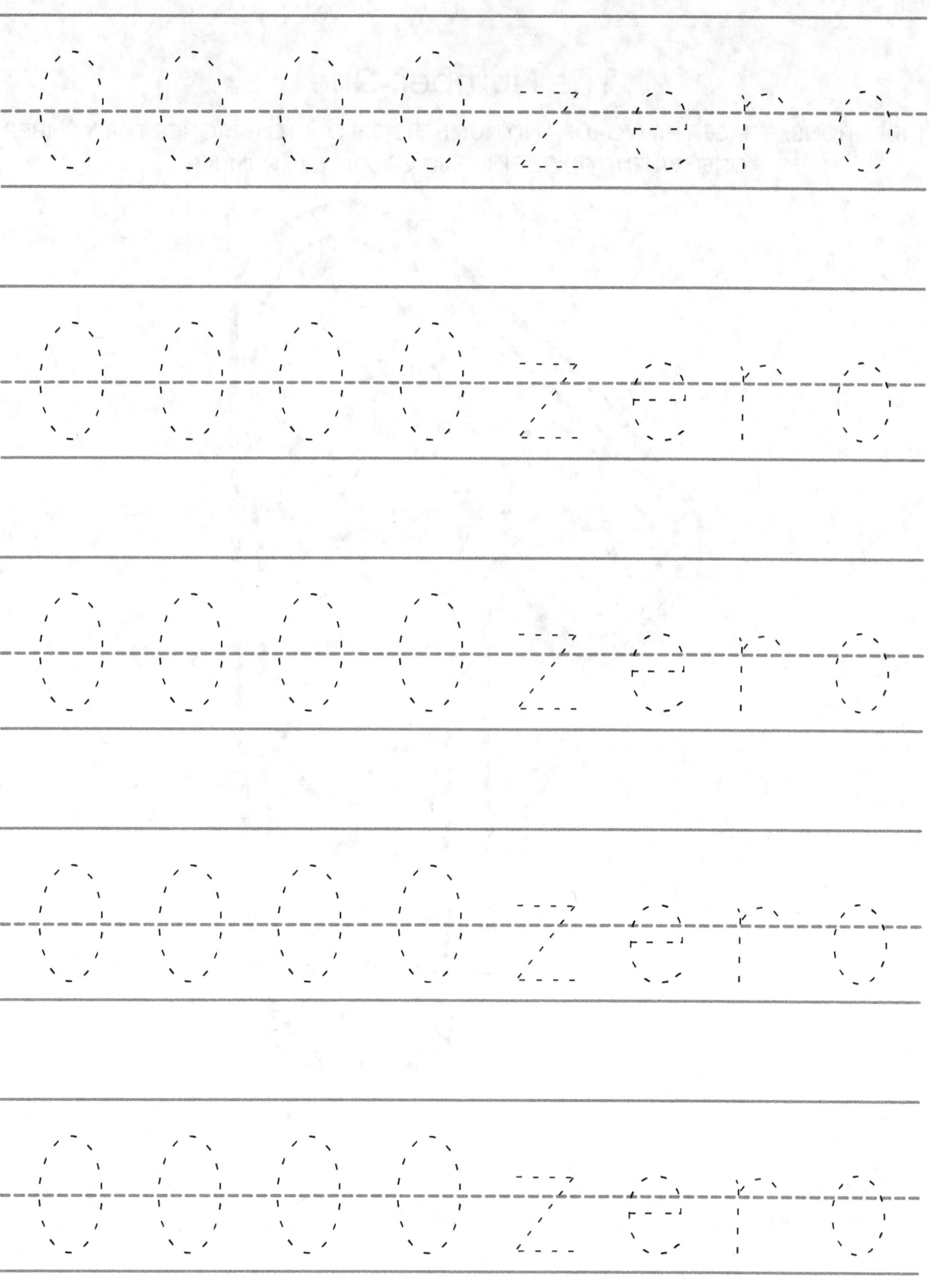

The Number One

DIRECTIONS: TRACE THE WORDS AND NUMBERS BELOW TO PRACTICE THE NUMBER ONE! WHEN YOU'RE FINISHED COLOR THE NUMBER.

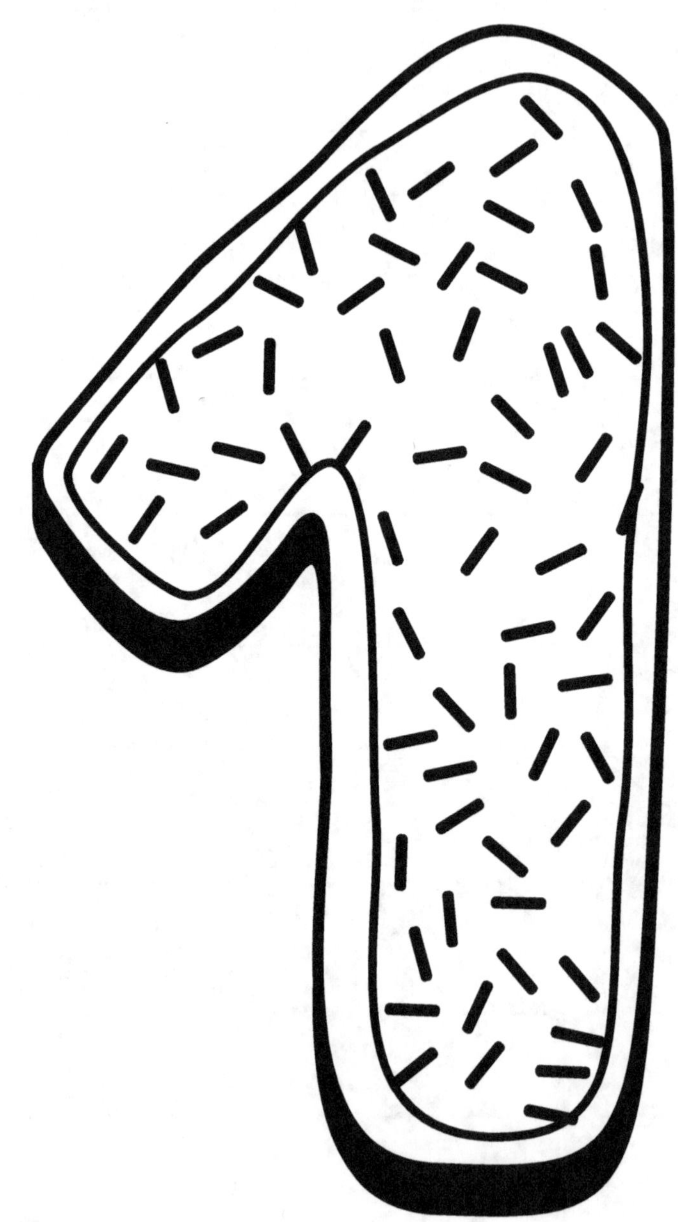

1 1 1 1 1   one

1 1 1 1 one

1 1 1 1 one one one

1 1 1 1 one one

1 1 1 1 one

1 1 1 1 one

The Number Two

DIRECTIONS: TRACE THE WORDS AND NUMBERS BELOW TO PRACTICE THE NUMBER TWO! WHEN YOU'RE FINISHED COLOR THE NUMBER.

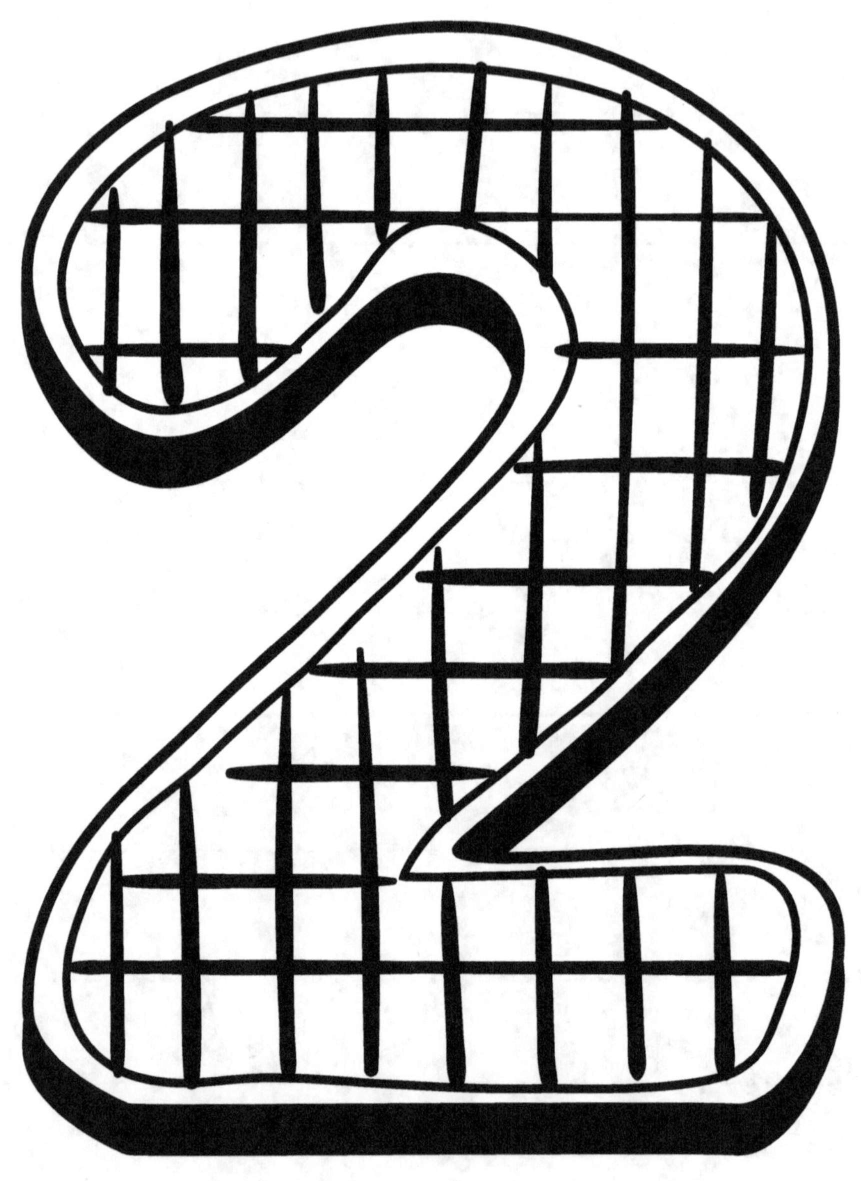

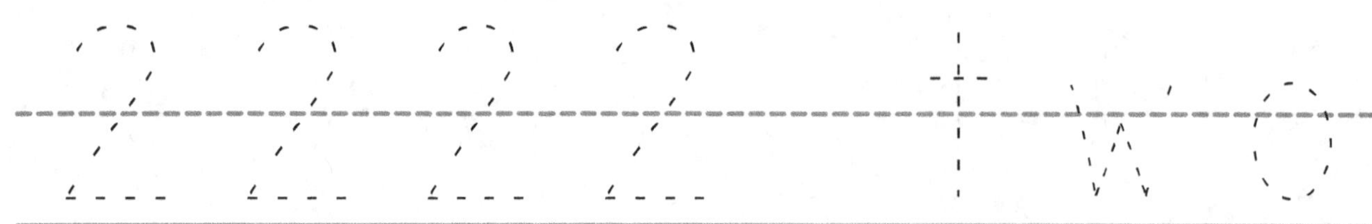

The Number Three

DIRECTIONS: TRACE THE WORDS AND NUMBERS BELOW TO PRACTICE THE NUMBER THREE! WHEN YOU'RE FINISHED COLOR THE NUMBER.

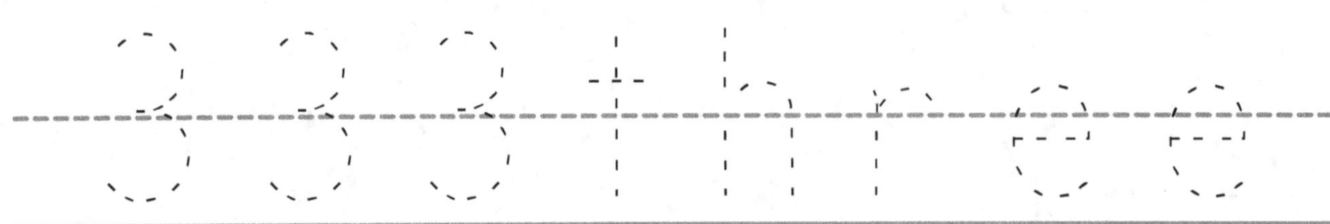

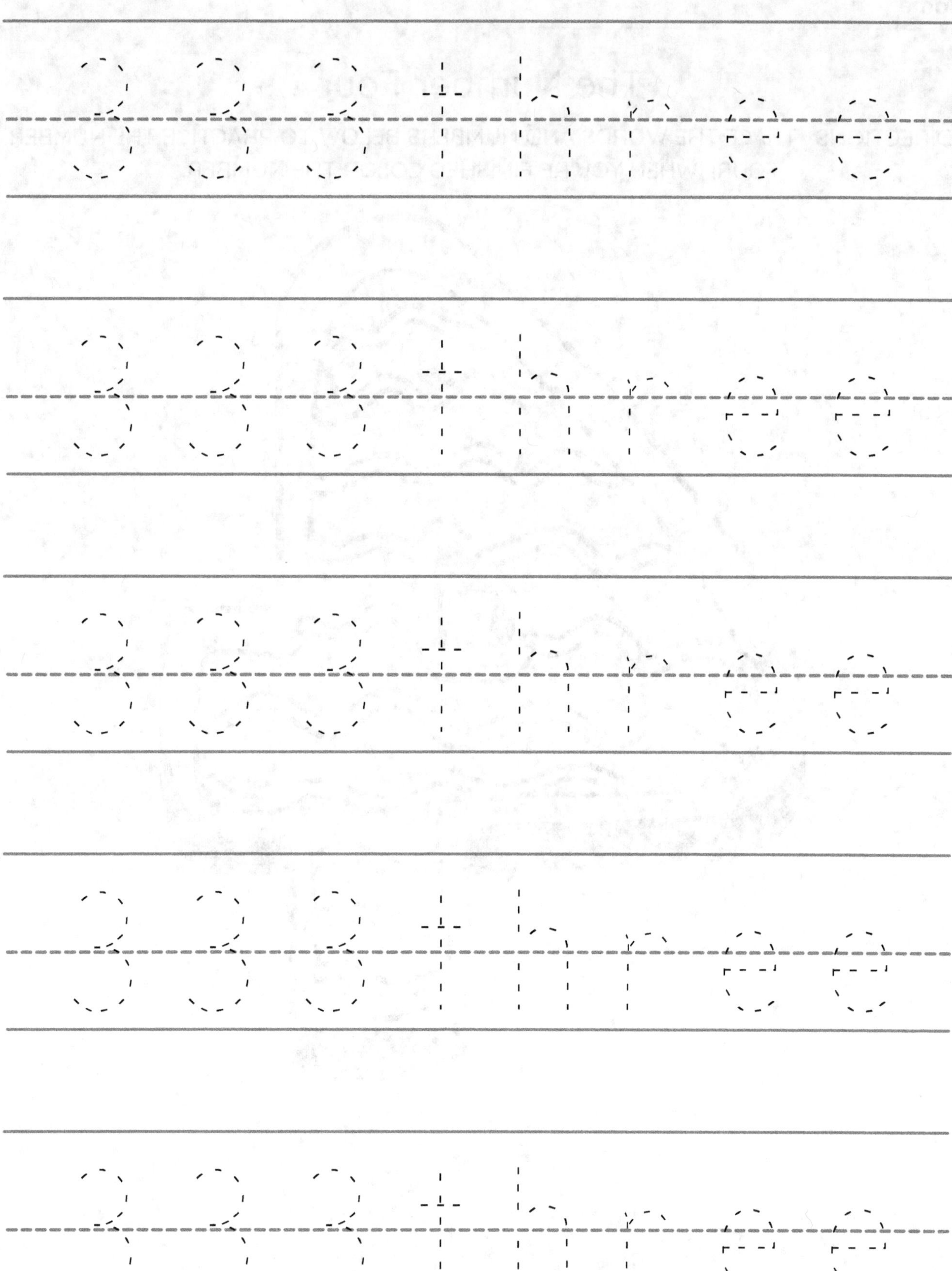

333three
333three
333three
333three
333three

The Number Four

DIRECTIONS: TRACE THE WORDS AND NUMBERS BELOW TO PRACTICE THE NUMBER FOUR! WHEN YOU'RE FINISHED COLOR THE NUMBER.

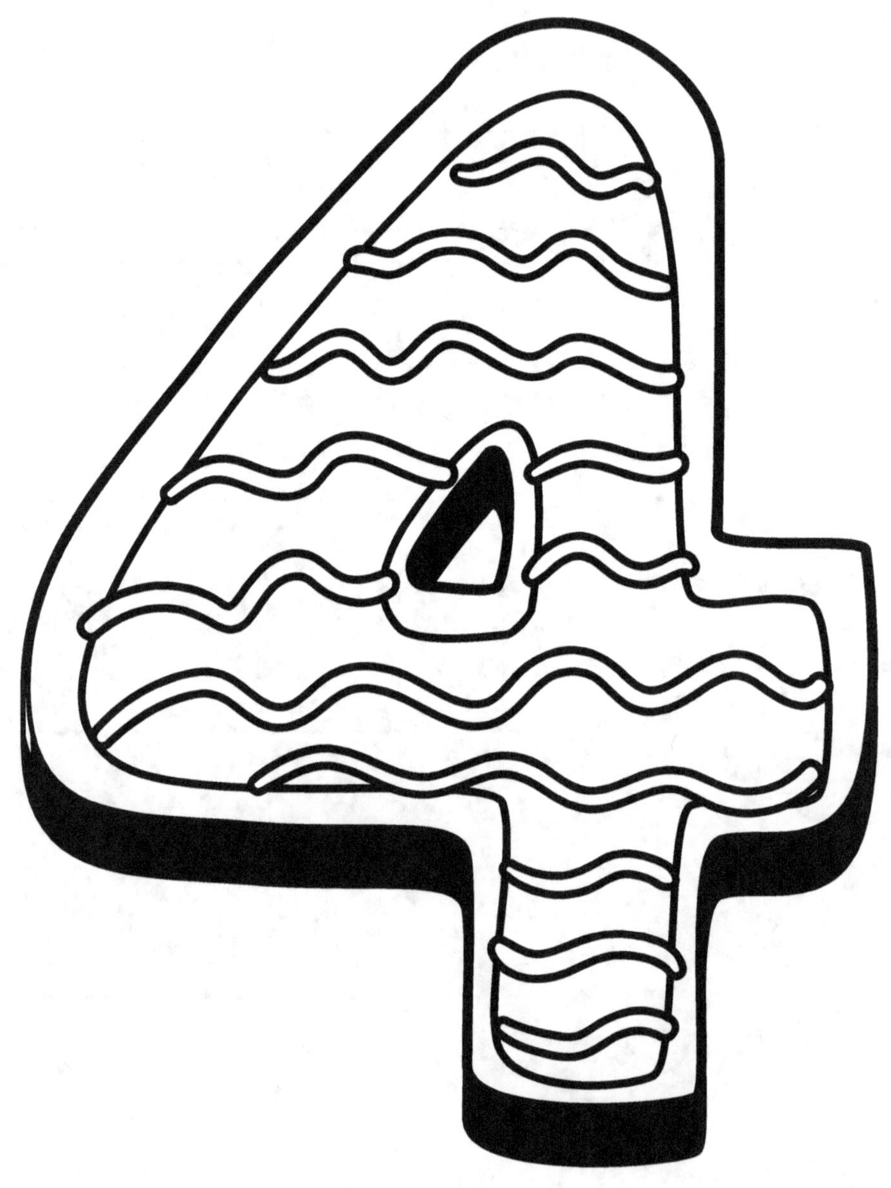

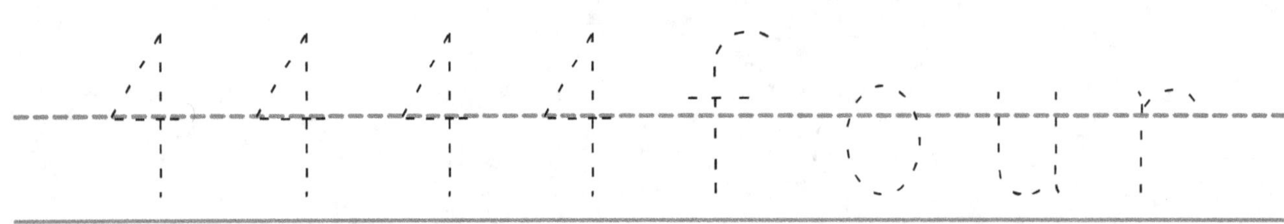

4 4 4 4 four

4 4 4 4 four

4 4 4 4 four

4 4 4 4 four

4 4 4 4 four

The Number Five

DIRECTIONS: TRACE THE WORDS AND NUMBERS BELOW TO PRACTICE THE NUMBER FIVE! WHEN YOU'RE FINISHED COLOR THE NUMBER.

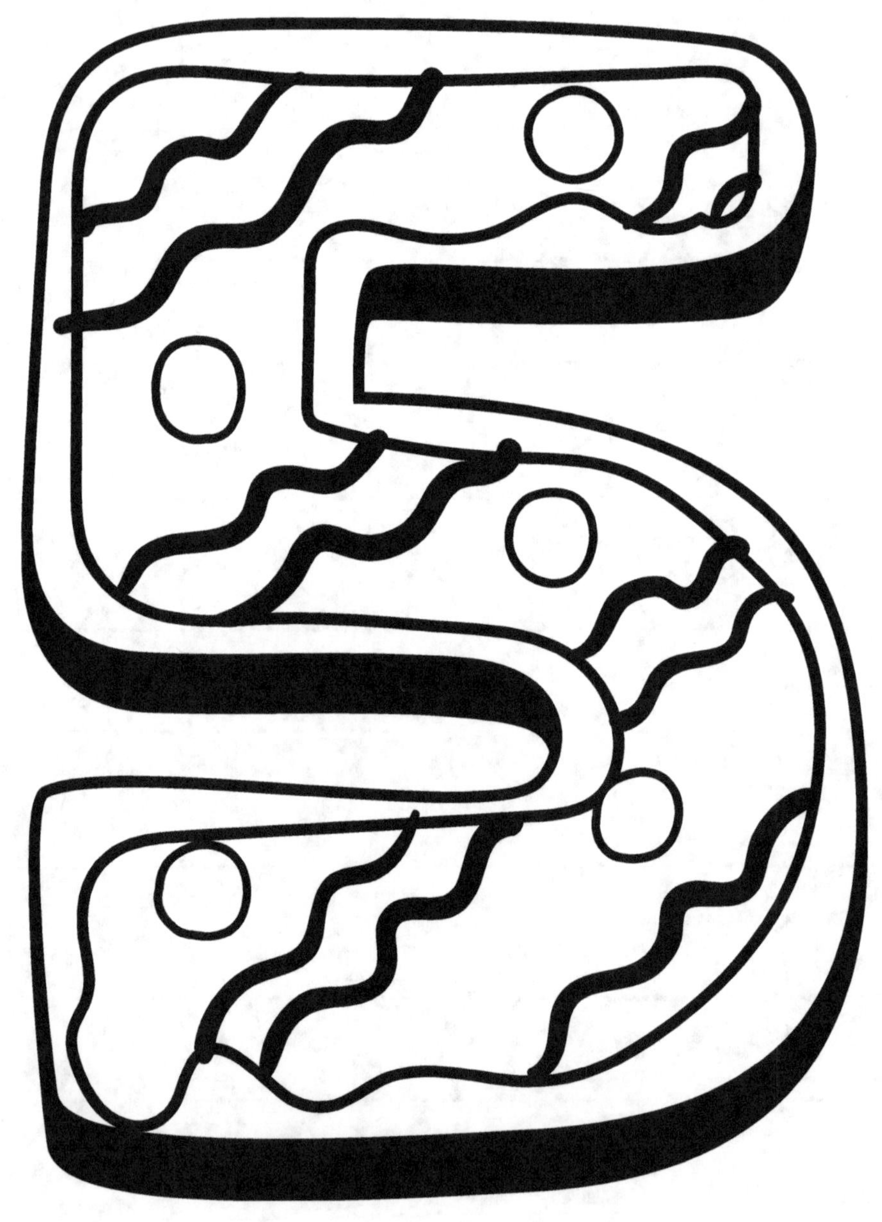

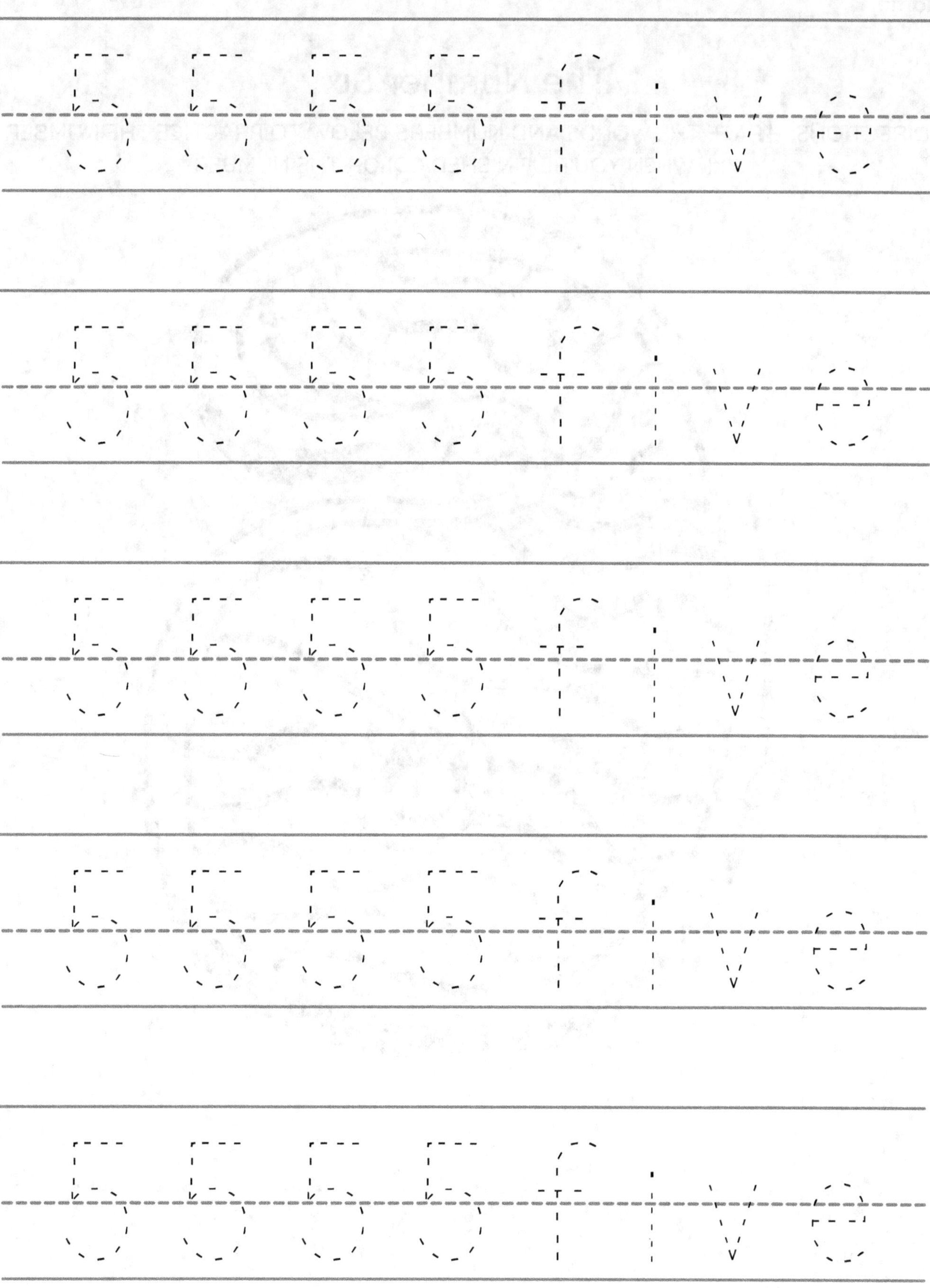

The Number Six

DIRECTIONS: TRACE THE WORDS AND NUMBERS BELOW TO PRACTICE THE NUMBER SIX! WHEN YOU'RE FINISHED COLOR THE NUMBER.

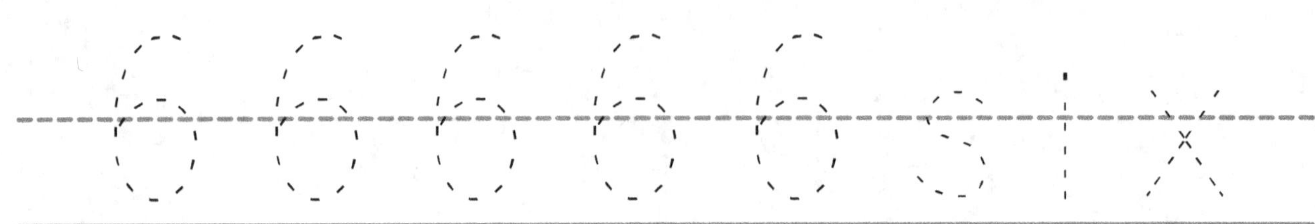

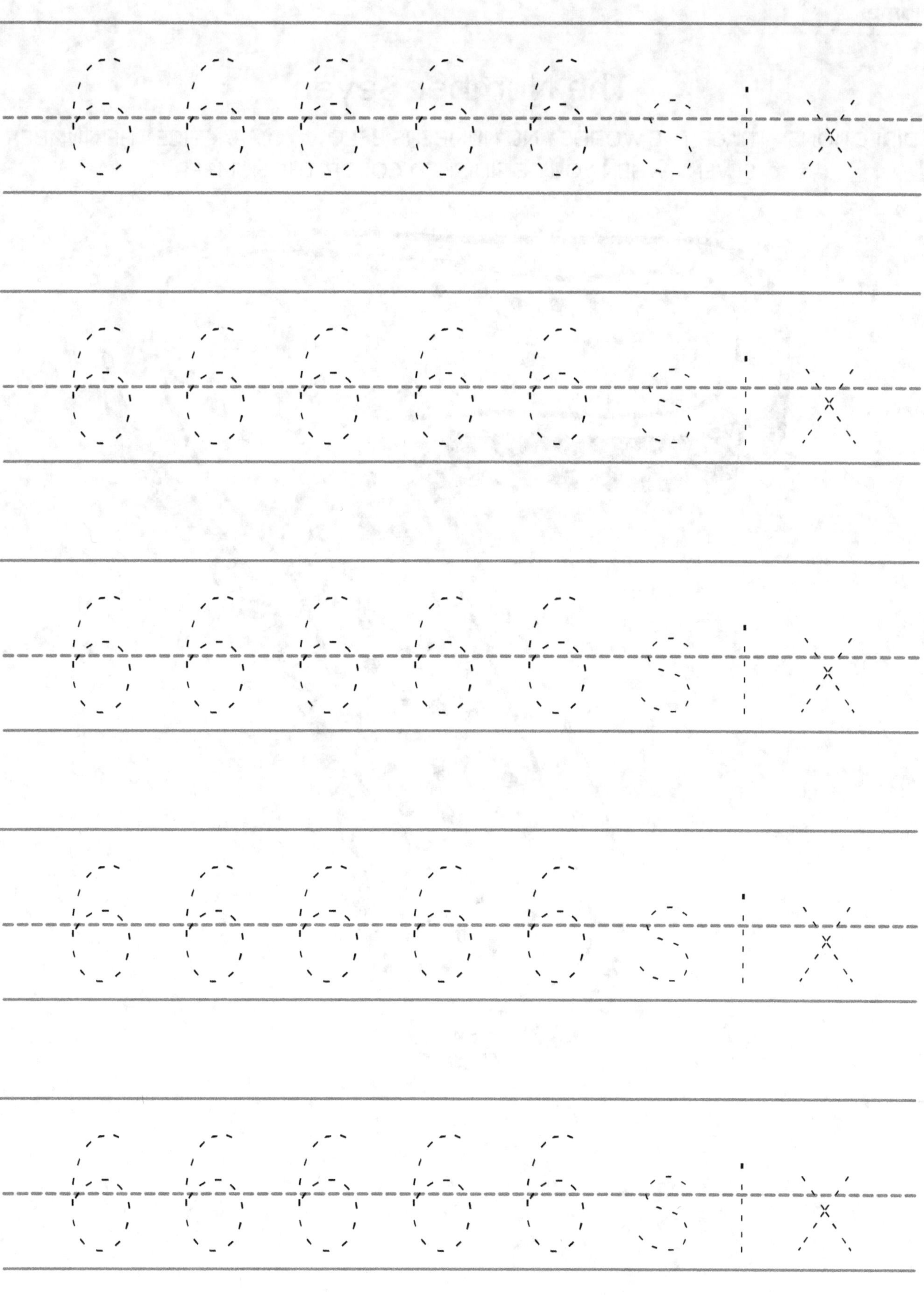
6 6 6 6 6 six
6 6 6 6 6 six
6 6 6 6 6 six
6 6 6 6 6 six
6 6 6 6 6 six

Name: ______________________

The Number Seven

DIRECTIONS: TRACE THE WORDS AND NUMBERS BELOW TO PRACTICE THE NUMBER SEVEN! WHEN YOU'RE FINISHED COLOR THE NUMBER.

7 7 7 seven

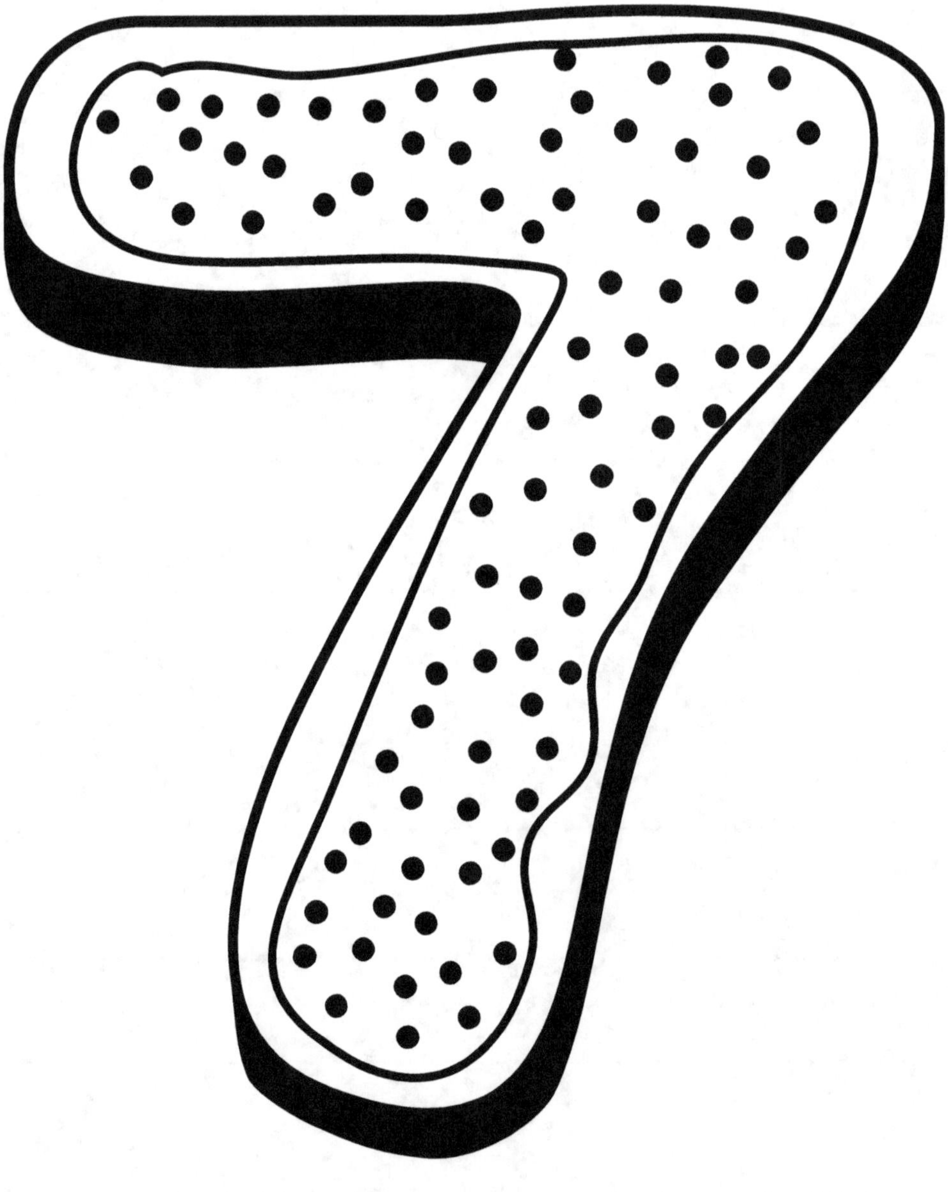

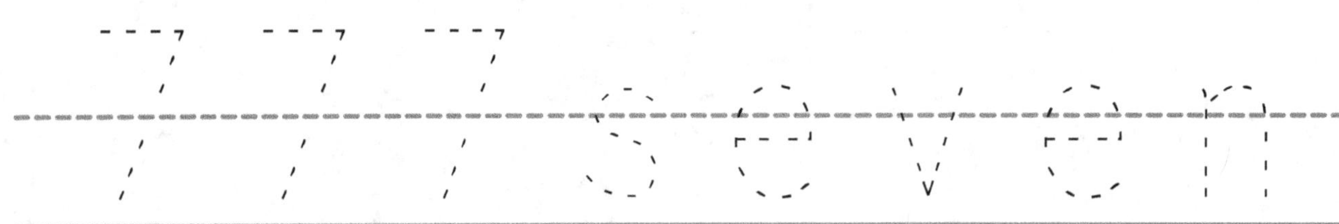

7 7 7 seven

7 7 7 seven

7 7 7 seven

7 7 7 seven

7 7 7 seven

Name: ______________________

The Number Eight

DIRECTIONS: TRACE THE WORDS AND NUMBERS BELOW TO PRACTICE THE NUMBER EIGHT! WHEN YOU'RE FINISHED COLOR THE NUMBER.

8 8 8 eight

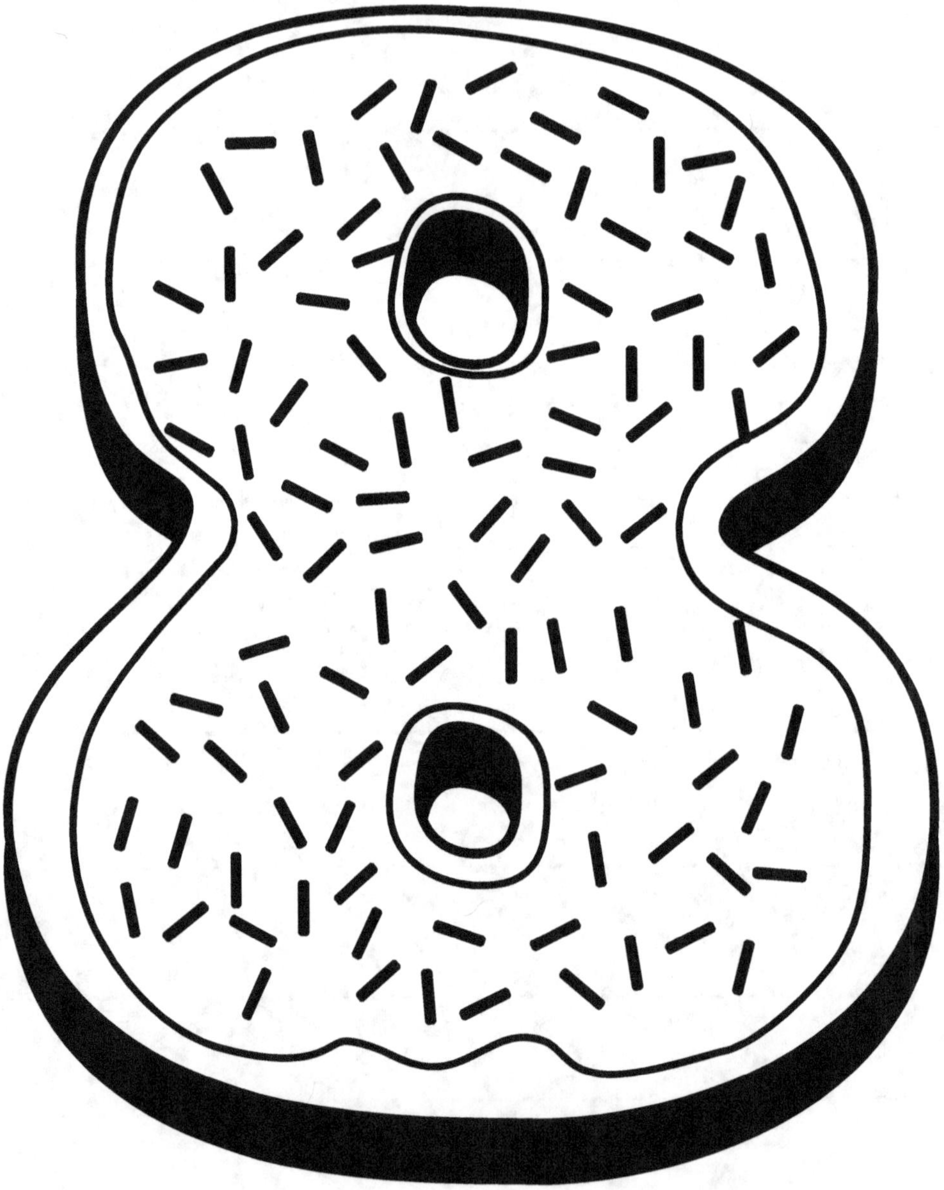

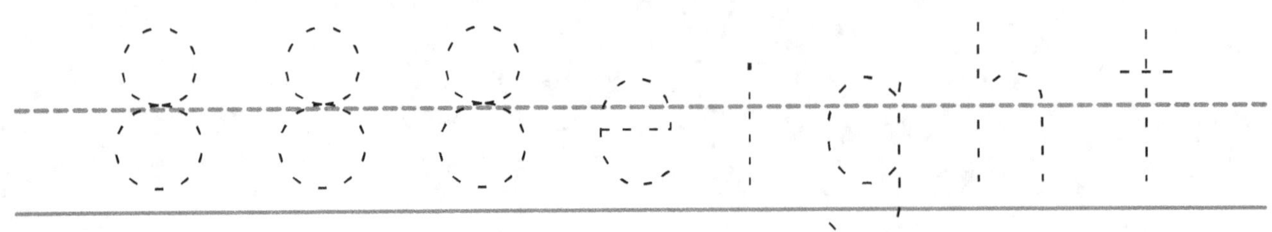

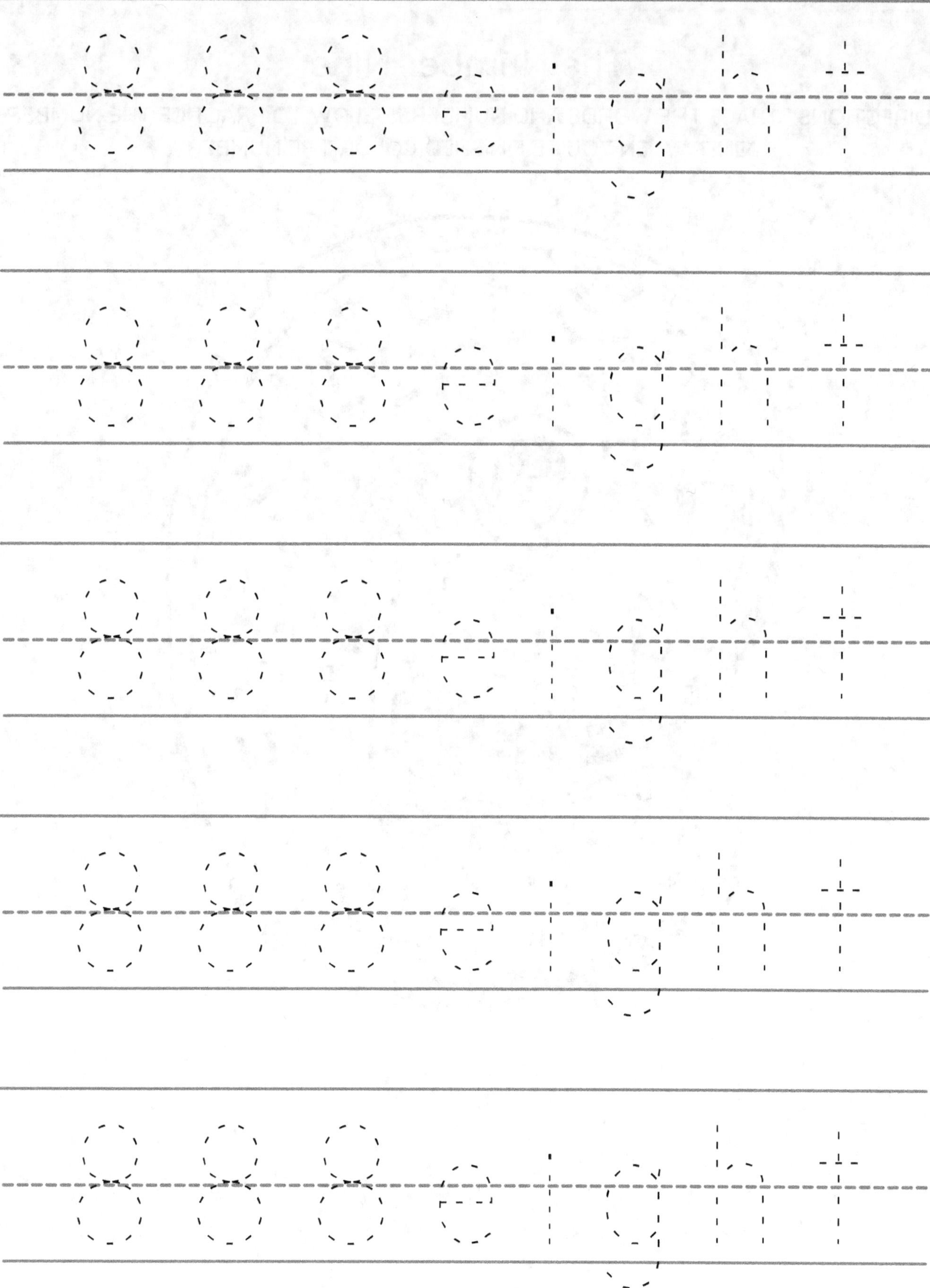

888 eight
888 eight
888 eight
888 eight
888 eight

The Number Nine

DIRECTIONS: TRACE THE WORDS AND NUMBERS BELOW TO PRACTICE THE NUMBER NINE! WHEN YOU'RE FINISHED COLOR THE NUMBER.

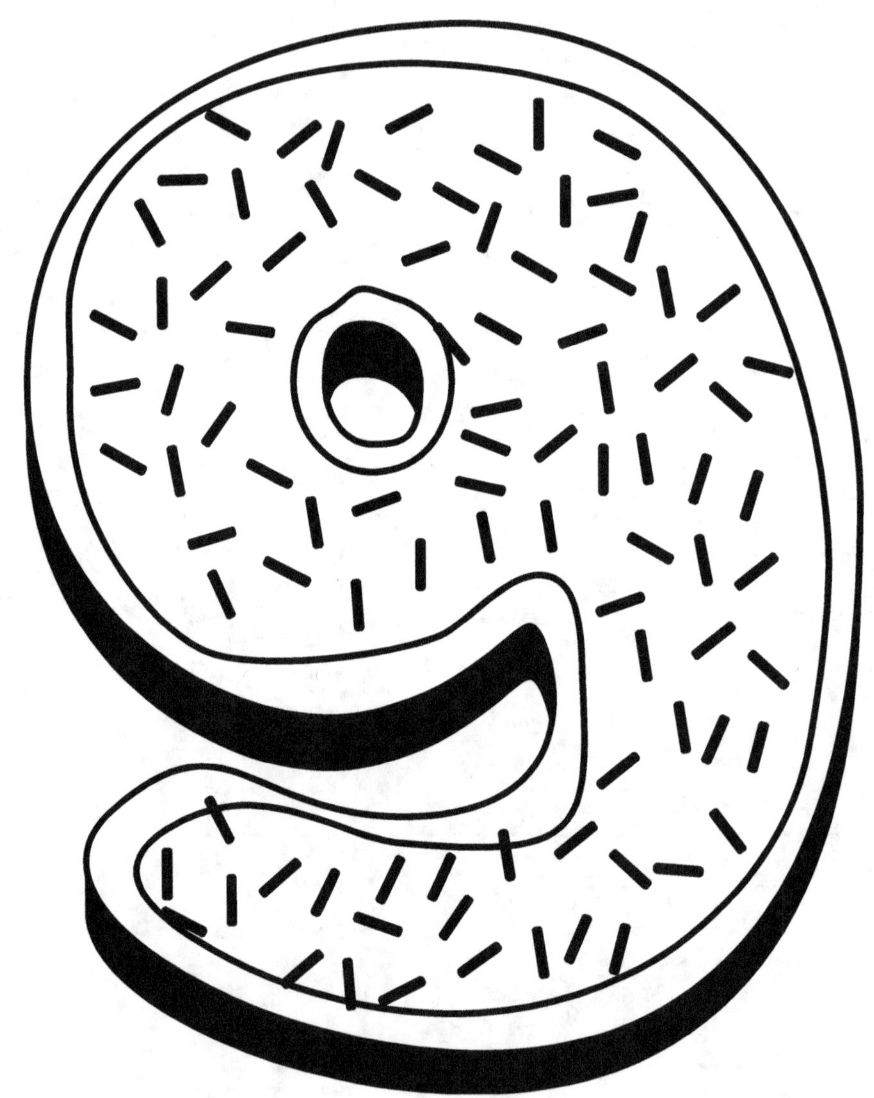

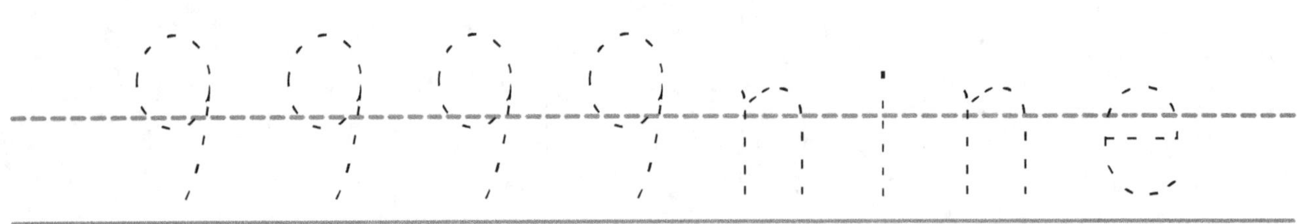

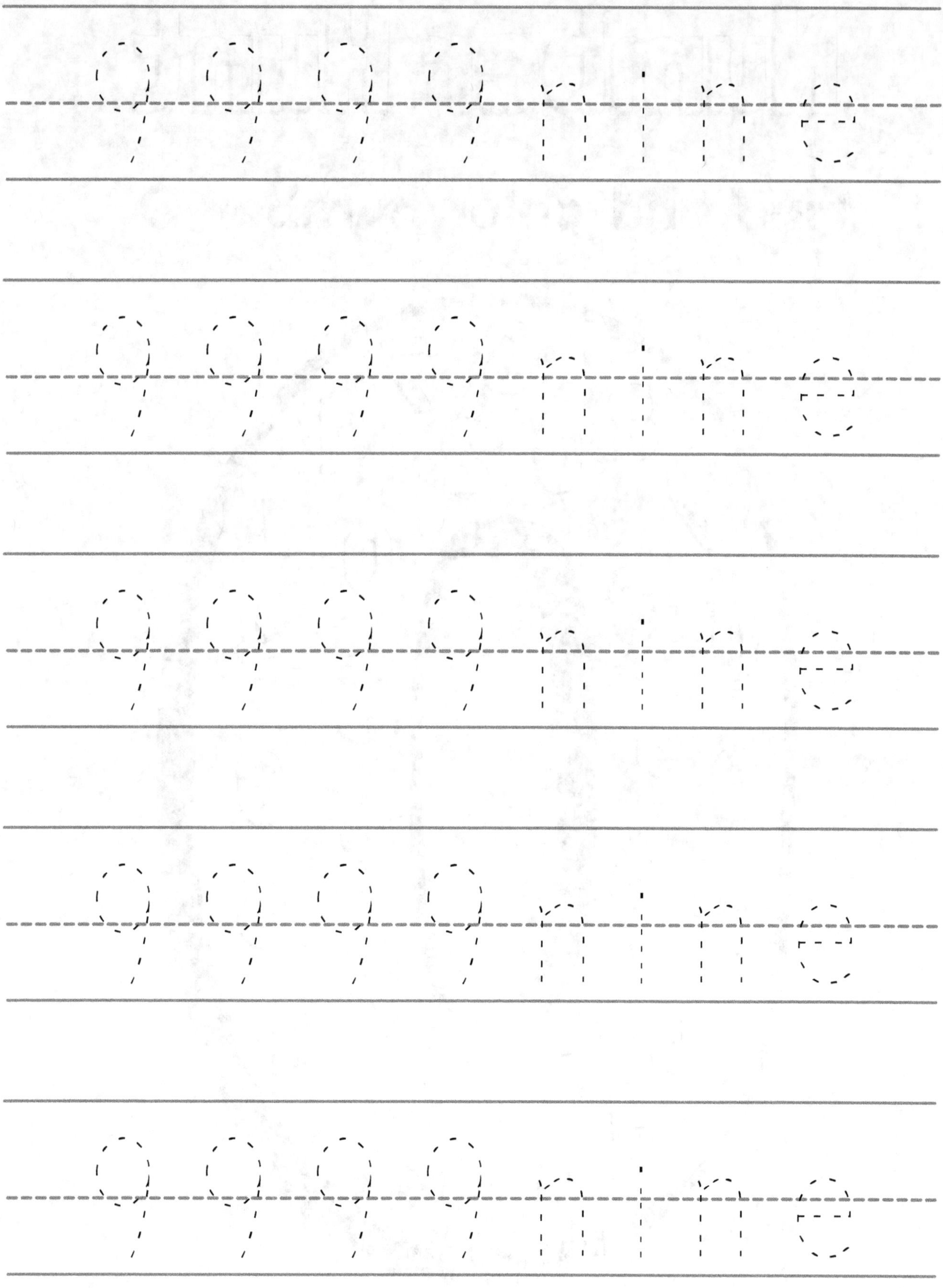
9 9 9 9 nine
9 9 9 9 nine
9 9 9 9 nine
9 9 9 9 nine
9 9 9 9 nine

Number Hunt

Find and color number O

Number Hunt

Find and color number 1

Number Hunt

Find and color number 2

Number Hunt

Find and color number 3

Number Hunt

Find and color number 4

Number Hunt

Find and color number 5

Number Hunt

Find and color number 6

Number Hunt

Find and color number 7

Number Hunt

Find and color number 8

Number Hunt

Find and color number 9

DIRECTIONS: TRACE THE NUMBERS IN THE CUPCAKES. IF TIME PERMITS, COLOR THE CUPCAKES.

DIRECTIONS: PRACTICE YOUR NUMBER WRITING WHEN FINISHED, COLOR
LUCKY'S HATS!

Number Practice 1-20

PRACTICE COUNTING. FILL IN THE BLANKS WITH THE MISSING NUMBERS.

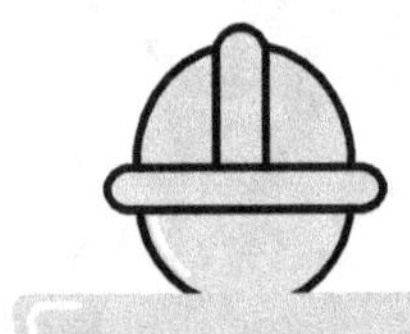

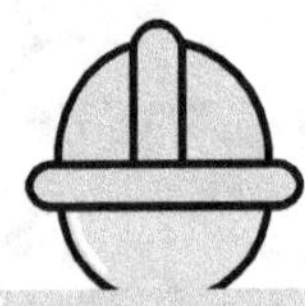

Directions: Help Lucky count his coins.

COUNTING PUZZLES

PRINT, LAMINATE, CUT & COUNT CUTE CATS

COUNTING PUZZLES

PRINT, LAMINATE, CUT & COUNT CUTE CATS

DIRECTIONS: COUNT THE HEARTS. WRITE THE NUMBER. WRITE THE WORD.